Selected Poems of Nancy Cunard

NANCY CUNARD was a poet, publisher, journalist and political activist. Born on 10 March 1896 in Nevill Holt, Leicestershire, Nancy was the great-granddaughter of shipping magnate Sir Samuel Cunard and the only child of Sir Bache and Lady Maud (Emerald) Cunard. Raised amid wealth and privilege, she began writing poetry during World War 1 and later authored two poetry collections, *Outlaws* (1921) and *Sublunary* (1923), as well as numerous chapbooks. As founder and editor of the Hours Press in La Chapelle-Réanville, France, Cunard was responsible for the appearance of major works by Modern writers including Samuel Beckett, Ezra Pound, and George Moore. In the 1930s she embarked on a life-long advocacy of political and social movements. During the Spanish Civil War and World War II, Cunard enlisted in the moral cause against Fascism and anti-imperialism, producing pamphlets in support of resistance movements and writing eye-witness reports for newspapers in the UK and the US. Following a relationship with the African American Jazz musician Henry Crowder, Cunard was essentially disinherited by her mother and spent the final decades of her life tirelessly advocating for her two great passions, poetry and social justice. Following a period of physical and mental breakdown, on 16 March 1965 she died alone in an open ward of the Hôpital Cochin, Paris.

SANDEEP PARMAR is Senior Lecturer in English Literature at the University of Liverpool. She is the author of the *Collected Poems of Hope Mirrlees* (2011) and *Reading Mina Loy's Autobiographies: Myth of the Modern Woman* (2014), a critical study of the modernist writer Mina Loy's literary archive. She has authored two books of poetry, *The Marble Orchard* (2012) and *Eidolon* (2015).

T0149127

FyfieldBooks aim to make available some of the great classics of British and European literature in clear, affordable formats, and to restore often neglected writers to their place in literary tradition.

FyfieldBooks take their name from the Fyfield elm in Matthew Arnold's 'Scholar Gypsy' and 'Thyrsis'. The tree stood not far from the village where the series was originally devised in 1971.

> *Roam on! The light we sought is shining still.*
> *Dost thou ask proof? Our tree yet crowns the hill,*
> *Our Scholar travels yet the loved hill-side*

from 'Thyrsis'

Selected Poems *of* Nancy Cunard

Edited by

SANDEEP PARMAR

Fyfield*Books*

CARCANET

First published in Great Britain in 2016 by

Carcanet Press Limited
Alliance House
Cross Street
Manchester M2 7AQ
www.carcanet.co.uk

A CIP catalogue record for this book is available
from the British Library, ISBN 9781784102364

The publisher acknowledges financial assistance
from Arts Council England

Typeset by XL Publishing Services, Exmouth

Contents

Introduction

For feminist literary critics, the resurrecting of marginal women writers calls for deft manoeuvring. An indelicate, exceptionalist gesture in favour of forgotten female genius inevitably fails. One has only to witness how 'neglected' women writers are set within scholarly histories of existing artistic constellations to see how their lives, influences, works – even their physical bodies – enter into an imagined, evaluative male space. And yet, the indisputable fact is that poet, publisher, journalist and editor Nancy Cunard (1896–1965) occupied a primary role in transatlantic modernism and the European avant-garde. Her myth persists: first glimpsed at the Bloomsbury literary salon of Edith, Sacheverell and Osbert Sitwell in the early decades of the twentieth century; later, as an author published by Virginia and Leonard Woolf's Hogarth Press; and then in accounts of and by her famous lovers Aldous Huxley, Michael Arlen, and Tristan Tzara, among others. As the visionary founder of the Hours Press, Cunard was the first to publish the twenty-three-year-old Samuel Beckett, as well as works by Richard Aldington, Ezra Pound and W. H. Auden. Cunard's reputation as striking artist's model and muse, and her lithe – probably anorexic – silhouette haunting Left Bank Paris in the 1920s and 30s, is remembered by most who have come across her remarkable likeness. As with so many of her female contemporaries, like Mina Loy and Djuna Barnes, the persistent image of Nancy Cunard is more myth than substance and somewhat self-cultivated. In a photograph taken by Man Ray in 1926, Cunard appears as a sharp, angled woman, up to her elbows in African ivory bracelets. Her pose is somewhere between alluring and defensive, and her side profile directs us towards an unknowable spectator just outside the frame. Worn through much of her life, these bracelets were a kind of personal armour and her astounding collection (much of which was stolen during World War II) testifies to her vulnerability as much as her tireless battles against social and political injustice. One hope of this volume of Cunard's poetry is to mediate the gaze of readers and modernist scholars between her compelling public image and her wide-ranging and extraordinary literary oeuvre.

Indian novelist Mulk Raj Anand recounts meeting Nancy Cunard in London in the 1920s with the biographer Catherine Carswell. Expressing surprise at finding her in a café called Whyte-lady's, Cunard retorts that she has already convinced the owner to rename it Black and White, and that she will invite the famous black American actor Paul Robeson to its inauguration. Cunard's mix of mischief and grandeur in this scene belies her serious life-long dedication to anti-Fascist, anti-racist and anti-imperial causes. According to Anand's memoir, *Conversations in Bloomsbury*, Cunard was deeply sympathetic to his views of the British Raj: he was beaten and imprisoned for taking part in Gandhi's resistance movement just before the Amritsar massacre in 1919. Cunard must have been reflecting on her own life when she replied, bending her head thoughtfully, 'Nothing like a personal insult to make you into a rebel!'[1] Cunard's public rebellion against the values and ambivalence of her own social class and nationality complicates her legacy, as one whose association with artistic and literary circles was peripheral and selective. From the 1920s to the 1940s, she appears and then unexpectedly vanishes from the frame of transatlantic modernism. During these years, Cunard reincarnated herself from rebellious heiress to writer, social activist, and avant-garde publisher. As the great-granddaughter of the Cunard shipping-line founder Samuel Cunard, Nancy could not avoid her association with one of the most famous families in the world. Her story begins with a privileged childhood and adolescence, gaily photographed at the races alongside the daughters of great men, then moves to a literary career marked by travel and social activism in the Spanish Civil War and for the French resistance. Through three major wars, Cunard championed art as the antidote to world chaos.

Cunard's Hours Press, which mostly operated between 1928 and 1931 in Paris and La Chapelle-Réanville, was looted and her home destroyed by German troops and pillaged by her French neighbours under the encouragement of the town's mayor. Books, letters, and artworks were lost – troops put eleven bullet holes through her Tanguy landscape and bayoneted her portrait by Eugene McCown – and many of Cunard's precious ivory bracelets were carried off.[2] Hence much of Cunard's correspondence with the key writers of her era no longer exists. Her archived notebooks bear traces of her end as an isolated, disinherited idealist, jotting out quick, dark and observant poems standing at a window or in the TV room of London's Holloway Sanatorium after being declared legally insane in 1960. Tragically, Cunard spent her final erratic days wandering the streets of Paris, where she was found weighing no more than twenty-six kilograms. On 17 March 1965 she died alone in the public ward of the charitable Hôpital Cochin in Paris.

Born in 1896 at Neville Holt, a thirteen-thousand-acre estate in rural Leicestershire, England, Nancy was the only child of Sir Bache Cunard and Maud Burke, a wealthy American who would later restyle herself as the flamboyant socialite Lady Emerald Cunard. Theirs was a marriage of convenience – Bache had forsaken the family business and was living as a country gentleman. Needing a wife to support his bucolic lifestyle, his title (that of a Baronet granted by Queen Victoria to his grandfather) lured in the beautiful and much younger Maud to a role in the British establishment. Becoming Lady Cunard, Maud gained much-craved social legitimacy and secured herself access to British royalty (Maud would later, unwisely, become the close confident of Wallis Simpson). The loveless marriage of Cunard's parents was wholly apparent to Nancy from a very young age: Maud's eventual separation from Nancy's father and her high-profile relationships with the writer George Moore ('G. M.') and the composer Thomas Beecham undoubtedly added to what must have been an emotionally deprived childhood. However, Nancy's access to literature in both French and English, the highly intellectual conversation of adults via her mother's salons (attended by artists and politicians such as Max Beerbohm, Somerset Maugham, the Balfours, the Asquiths, and Lady Randolph Churchill), and international travel during her childhood, provided strong foundations for an increasingly worldly and itinerant life. She was not only presented at Court in 1914, she was also the favourite dancing partner of none other than Edward the Prince of Wales (who she found boring, unsophisticated and 'physically slow to mature').[3] Nancy's early prewar years as a spoiled debutante – part of a 'Corrupt Coterie' of young aristocrats, artists and writers including Lady Diana Manners and the poet Iris Tree, among others – ended with her introduction to the avant-garde circles of wartime London, populated by Ezra Pound and Wyndham Lewis. Pound was already known to Cunard's mother, as was T. S. Eliot; both had been guests at her Cavendish Square soirées, including the first performance of W. B. Yeats's play *At the Hawk's Well* in London in 1916.[4] That same year, Lady Cunard had also helped Pound secure a Civil List grant for James Joyce. Years later, on hearing of Eliot's death in January 1965, Nancy wrote a poem titled 'Letter' (published here for the first time) in which she recalled first meeting him at one of her mother's society balls.

> We met, you and I, first, that summer night of 1922,
> At a ball – You in 'smoking', I in a panniered dress
> Of Poiret: red, gold with cascading white tulle on the hips.
> The P. of W. was there (so polite, lovely face) and we danced
> together;
> The hostess, that small termagent, in all her glitterings,
> Brilliant was she, the hostess, at this sort of thing.
>
> Bored by it all was I. After many dances we went down
> Alone, by the grand staircase to the supper room.
> It was *then*; Eliot, you came in, alone too, for the first time to my
> eyes;
> Well-advised of you was I, already somewhat versed in you:
> I mean *Prufrock*.

Hindsight softened her impressions of the Prince of Wales (Edward VIII) and her estranged mother – and quite possibly of Eliot himself, whose later-life conservative, religious, pro-royalist nationalism she would have despised. In 'Letter' she goes on to describe a gin-fuelled tryst with Eliot in front of a gas fire in a private room above Soho's Eiffel Tower restaurant. Cunard sent the poem to Eliot's close friend, the editor John Hayward, on hearing of Eliot's death, but did not receive an immediate reply. About a week later, she chivvied a response: 'You will have had my poem to you on Eliot by now. I wonder, will you be liking it or not? I hope you will be liking it. Oh, how it surged up, written, all the first part, standing up after lunch, with the usual interruptions, written on further, immediately later; corrected as best I might later yet.'[1] Hayward's eventual reply was discouraging: Cunard wrote back that she would keep the poem private, as she had always intended. 'As for the personal element in my "Letter" to you (called "Letter" on purpose), *I meant it that way*. So you understood. I wondered, thinking you would. So we agree – this a "Letter" just for you and me.' 'Letter' is an homage to both Eliot's effect on Cunard's early poetry and to his great stature in later life. It is also marvellously coy about the night they shared together: 'Not every life-moment's recalled, though all of that night certainly is... / Not every moment goes into one's histories, / Be they written, or even, spoken.' No doubt Hayward feared the potentially scandalous revelation of a kind of intimacy between Eliot and Cunard, hence his act of suppression. Reading the poem now, in light of their shared responses to World War I and the shared high-modernist aesthetics of *The Waste Land* and *Parallax* especially, their diverging styles in later life are even more stark. Cunard's absorption in French Surrealism in the 1930s, and her fervent activist (at times anarchic) political poetry, contrasts sharply with Eliot's Anglicisation and the religious themes of his *Four Quartets*. The two corresponded little during the 1920s and 1930s; mostly Cunard wrote asking Eliot to contribute work to the Hours Press or to one of her many projects. Unbeknownst to Cunard, T. S. Eliot made a cruel and inaccurate caricature of her as the whoreish 'Fresca' in drafts of *The Waste Land*, a seventy-two-line section wisely redacted by Ezra Pound from the final manuscript. Mimicking the style of Jonathan Swift's 'The Lady's Dressing Room', Eliot mocks Cunard's intellect and literary ambition:

When restless nights distract her brain from sleep
She may as well write poetry, as count sheep.
And on those nights when Fresca lies alone,
She scribbles verse of such a gloomy tone
That cautious critics say, her style is quite her own.[6]

Nevertheless, Cunard's admiration of Eliot's poem 'The Love Song of J Alfred Prufrock' initially drew her to him, though their 'affair' was short-lived and judging from her portrayal in *The Waste Land* it is not difficult to guess why: Eliot clearly paints Cunard as predatory. Yet their loose friendship appears to have been significant enough for him to gift Cunard a handwritten copy of his poem 'Gerontion', the first and more innocuous appearance of Lady Fresca, which she treasured for decades.

Cunard's earliest published poems were written at the start of World War I. Some of these appeared in *The Eton College Chronicle* between 1915 and 1916, then edited by Cunard's cousin Victor Cunard. 'Prayer' is her very first published poem, a sort of individualist anti-prayer for self-preservation: 'Oh God, make me incapable of prayer, / Too brave for supplication'. The nine-line poem uncannily prophecies her legacy as a writer, editor and activist: 'Make me symbolically iconoclast, / The ideal Antichrist, the Paradox.' Her two sonnets 'Soldiers Fallen in Battle' and 'Sonnet', published together in June 1916, reflect her wartime anguish more generally, but also personally for those friends who never returned from the Front: 'all men soon forget that they are dead, / And their dumb names unwrit on memory's page.' Like the war poets Siegfried Sassoon and Wilfred Owen, Cunard criticises the living as 'the morning crowd, / Who walked like hypocrites, with bare heads bowed.' Sometimes her wartime sense of exasperation and despair was self-directed, as in her poem 'Remorse', published in Edith Sitwell's 1916 *Wheels* anthology (named after Cunard's poem of the same title). Describing herself as ashamed and silent, Cunard begins, 'I have been wasteful, wanton, foolish, bold'. Already one senses her political consciousness and her emerging disconnect with the values of 'civilised' society brewing in these poems and in her first two poetry collections, *Outlaws* (1921) and *Sublunary* (1923). A review of *Wheels* in the *Times Literary Supplement* notes the 'dark and boding phantoms' oppressing Cunard's mind – other contributors to the first (of six) cycle of *Wheels* include the three Sitwells, Iris Tree, Helen Rootham and James Arnold. The TLS reviewer also notes the volume's pervasive lack of hope in the present and future. According to Cunard's biographer, a combination of 'survivor's guilt' on seeing wounded soldiers returning from the Front and the death of one of Cunard's lovers (a Grenadier

Guards officer named Peter Broughton Adderly with whom she had a five-day romance) most probably led Cunard to suddenly and ill-advisedly marry a soldier with whom she had little in common. Nancy Cunard and Sydney Fairbairn, an Australian officer also in the Guards, married on November 15, 1916. They separated twenty months later and divorced finally in 1925.[7]

Cast into the ring with Cunard's later work, her first two full-length collections are comparatively sentimental and at times archaic, making use of inverted syntax, emotive personifications of 'Death', 'Night', 'Love', 'Joy', 'Time' and 'Sin', as well as traditional form (the sonnet) and regular end-rhyme. Although images of romance, loss, and modern warfare run throughout *Outlaws*, Cunard hadn't yet found a modern language to transmit the horrors of conflict.

> And yet we live while others die for us;
> Live in the glory of sweet summer, still
> Knowing not death, but knowing that life will
> Be merciless to them – and so to us.
> Blood lies too rich on many battlefields,
> Too many crowns are made for solemn sorrow;
> We rise from weeping, and the cruel morrow
> Has nought, but to a further sorrow yields.
>
> (from 'War')

As she wrote to Pound, many years later in 1946, excoriating him at length for his Fascism, she would learn from her war experience and exposure to battle that 'War is not abstract.'[8]

In 1920 Cunard left London to live in Paris. Much of *Sublunary* is set in France – Paris and Provence – and the Basque region of northern Spain. In 1922, after a serious illness that led to a hysterectomy, she set off on a walking tour of Southern France with Ezra Pound, who had visited her in Paris during her convalescence. Only two letters from Pound survive in Cunard's archive: one from the 1930s addressed intimately to 'Avril' (as he called her), and another from his incarceration at St Elizabeth's Hospital in response to Cunard's vocal disgust for his Italian radio broadcasts. Cunard and Pound became lovers in 1922, and her biographer rightly reads *Sublunary* as reflective of Cunard's adoration of him and his connection to the French landscape.[9]

'Shall We Forget?' indicates the tenuousness of their brief affair, already anticipating separation – Pound was by this time married to Dorothy Shakespear and living with her in Rapallo.

> When we must go our ways no more together
> After this shortening time that love has given
> Our hearts to meet, remember that day of driven
> And wayward rains, soft lulls in the wild weather,
> And we on the road, full-hearted with mute lips
> Masking the sorrow each should have of each
> Once all things told. [...]

Although their 'delicate vow of love' is 'wrought with uncertainty', this and other poems in *Sublunary*, such as 'The April Hour', suggest that their journey, the cyclical seasons, and the renewed promises of spring ordain their fated union.

'From Afar' and 'I Think of You' date from Cunard's separation from Pound later that year and are absorbed by nostalgia and solitude. And *Sublunary* marks a departure of another kind: Cunard's poetry after 1923 shifts towards more of what she would refer to as an 'experimental' (and, by her definition, non-commercial) poetics, which she aimed to foster through the Hours Press. Although contemporary readers may see *Parallax* and her poems written during the 1940s as invested in conventional syntax and meaning, traces of high modernist and avant-garde lineation, attention to high and low forms of diction, polyvocality, itinerancy and intertextual allusion point most convincingly to echoes of Eliot's *The Waste Land* and to the influence of French Surrealism and the political, temporal inflections of some modernist poetry. Even *Sublunary*'s 'Ballad of 5 Rue De L'Etoile' strongly echoes Eliot's 'Prufrock'.

> I'll tell you how the women come and go,
> Seemly and neat – for love will have it so;

Love that must climb some narrow midnight stair
Up several floors, demands good comfort there,
And comfort finding maybe will return –

After *Sublunary* Cunard finally abandons this hesitant, sentimental aesthetic and comes of age: 'I am in years almost the century's child, / At grips with still the same uncertainty / That was attendant to me at the school.' ('Adolescence') In the coming years, and through experiences of war and injustice, she would level her poetic aims away from the personal and her own past in order to give voice to those suffering social and political crisis.

Virginia and Leonard Woolf advised Cunard against starting her own publishing press unless she did not mind her hands always being black with printer's ink. Cunard wrote in her memoir, *These Were the Hours*, 'This seemed no deterrent. And it was with curiosity I looked at my black and greasy hands after the first go with the inking table.'[10] When it came to publishing *Parallax* in 1925, two years after having typeset the Hogarth edition of *The Waste Land* (1923) and long after Virginia's famous struggle with Hope Mirrlees's complex typography in *Paris* (1920), the Woolfs were well prepared for the poem's long lines and liberal spacing. Reviewers of *Parallax* noted the poem's self-confessed similarity with Eliot's work: 'T. S. Eliot is the first who heard the new music in its full harmony. Miss Cunard has caught strains of it too. She is not piping over again Mr Eliot's tune [but] adding her own motifs and orchestration to the general theme.' The same reviewer notes that Cunard displays an understanding of the 'zeitgeist'.[11] The *Nation*'s reviewer also noted the example of Eliot's poem but argued for *Parallax*'s individuality and subtle emotionality. Indeed, the Eliotic echoes are present and unmasked, and both poems move through space and time with a similar expressive restlessness (some of which Pound edited out of *The Waste Land*). The idea of parallax – the appearence of movement in external objects caused by the movement of the viewer – is an apt metaphor for the movement of Cunard's speaker through cities and rural landscapes. Following the 'poet-fool' through the streets of London, then south through France and Italy, the drift (and backward drift to London, 'the hideous wall, the jail of what I am') re-treads Cunard's move away from England and her travels with (and without, but longing for) Pound. Cunard's many Eliotic constructions of postwar London include:

> By the Embankment I counted the grey gulls
> Nailed to the wind above a distorted tide.
> On discreet waters
> In Battersea I drifted, acquiescent.

We encounter the Prufrockian rhythms of Cunard's repeated 'immortal Question' amid the mundane

> Habit of days,
> The yawning visits, the forced revisitations.
> Oh very much the same, these faces and places,
> These meals and conversations [...]
> [...]
> 'Hail partner, that went as I
> In towns, in wastes – I, shadow,
> Meet with you – I that have walked with recording eyes
> Through a rich bitter world, and seen
> The heart close with the brain, the brain crossed by the heart –
> > I that have made, seeing all,
> > Nothing, and nothing kept, nor understood
> > Of the empty hands, the hands impotent through time
> > > that lift and fall
> > Along a question – [...]'

Startlingly concrete images ('Two old women drinking on a cellar floor / Huddled, with a beerish look at the scavenging rat') anchor the listless motion of the wandering poet engaged in the struggle between life, art, and nihilism. Crucially, a fluidity of pronouns and perspectives reappears throughout Cunard's work but takes on a wider purpose as it becomes more overtly political. As Jane Dowson has written, referring to Cunard's poem 'Wheels', 'she bridges personal and public discourses by moving between first person singular and plural'.[12]

After the 1930s, Cunard's poetry blurs the personal and political in a way that anticipates postwar protest and feminist poetry especially. *Parallax*, and her poems from World War II and the Spanish Civil War, are the best measure of Cunard's poetic genius, even though her published and unpublished work after 1925 would, until now, remain largely uncollected. Carefully preserved drafts and hand-bound manuscripts of these early poems contrast sharply with the state of Cunard's later work in her archive, attesting to the relative instability of those years.

The years after 1927 are characterised by Cunard's enormous *Negro* anthology project (1934), the Hours Press, her war journalism for various newspapers including despatches on Mussolini's annexation of Abyssinia for the American Negro Press and Spanish Civil War reports for the *Manchester Guardian*, and increasingly feverish international travel. Already inspired by Surrealism and its attraction to African 'primitive' art, Cunard set out to publish (by hand, on a two-hundred-year-old Belgian Mathieu press) 'contemporary poetry of an experimental kind – always very modern things, short pieces of fine quality that, by their nature, might have difficulty in finding commercial publishers'.[13] In 1929, struggling with the rural inconveniences of the farmhouse Le Puits Carré in La Chappelle-Réanville, Cunard moved the Hours Press to Paris, renting a small shop on the Rue Guenégaud, a minor street near the Left Bank's Rue de Seine. There she fell quickly into an active literary and artistic community, which included her lover Louis Aragon, whose meetings took place in local cafés Les Deux Magots and Café Flore, or at the Gallerie Surrealiste in the nearby Rue Jacques Callot. The Gallerie sold works by Francis Picabia, Picasso, Miro, Klee, Tanguy and Man Ray, as well as fetish objects and masks from Africa and Oceania. Cunard credits her fascination with African art to the abstract painter and photographer Curtis Moffat (husband of Iris Tree) who, around 1921, introduced her to what would become a life-long obsession. In her memoir of the Hours Press, Cunard recalls Arthur Symons bringing the sexologist Havelock Ellis to dine at her apartment on the Ile St Louis in 1926; she describes a then-unknown Samuel Beckett's submission to her publication prize; she lovingly recounts seeing many of her books from manuscript to the finished product. These years, which saw her tireless, expert production of the Press's twenty-four books and pamphlets by Ezra Pound (*A Draft of XXX Cantos*), Richard Aldington, Samuel Beckett (*Whoroscope*), Laura Riding, Robert Graves, and Havelock Ellis (*The Revaluation of Obscenity*), were among Cunard's most productive and happiest.

From the late 1920s Nancy Cunard's authorial self and poetic consciousness formulated itself in response to internationalism, cultural and racial otherness, as well as a strong rejection of the values of her social class and 'home' nation. Much of her activism has its origins in the political movements taken up by certain avant-gardes in the postwar generation, including her exposure to Aragon's interest in Communism (which Cunard did not subscribe to, ever suspicious of ideologies). However, it was the 'race question' in the United States that seems to have ultimately galvanised her passion for social justice. The complex and controversial publication history of Cunard's *Negro* anthology in 1934 – with its stated aim to record 'the struggles and achievements, the persecutions and the revolts' largely against 'the black race' in America and Europe – is well documented. One hundred and fifty voices contributed to the anthology in an editorial process that saw Cunard zig-zagging the Atlantic (from Europe to the United States and the West Indies) in support of her project. *Negro* included historical resources from the beginning of the slave trade to its abolition as well as expressions of black culture, religious belief and political aims produced by leading black writers and thinkers such as W. E. B. Dubois, James W. Ford, George Padmore, and Zora Neale Hurston, alongside several sympathetic white poets and writers. Designed as an indictment of America's legal and social divisions between races, and the legacy of transatlantic slavery, Cunard's book was meant to lead onto a second (unfulfilled) project: a poetry anthology titled *Revolution – the Negro Speaks*.

Presumably an expansion on the poetry from *Negro* by black poets (such as Countee Cullen and Langston Hughes), *Revolution* intended to celebrate 'the triumphant solution in the Russian

Soviets of race and class questions' and to denounce 'rival imperialisms and parallel class struggles' at the heart of racial oppression worldwide. Her call for submissions reads:

> Your Collaboration is wanted to make a short Symposium of Poetry: "Revolution – the Negro Speaks"
>
> Oppressed, despoiled, weighted down with the lies of his savagery and inferiority – since the first contacts of white men with black – slave at first, victim now, witness of rival imperialisms and parallel class-struggles, witness also of the triumphant solution in the Russian Soviets of race and class questions, the new Negro of today... how else than a revolutionary-born can he be?
>
> Let us make a record of the Negro's rising spirit against oppression. That this may have shape, and be more than an atmosphere of revolt, let us make it as much as possible a collection of poems inspired by some revolutionary event, some phase of the struggle in Negro history, past and present.
>
> Free verse, sonnet, ballad, lyric or folk-poem – no matter the form – but a call to freedom, now, or in the past.
>
> "Poets are the Trumpets that sing to Battle"
>
> No Poem should be longer than two typed pages at most.
>
> The editor's aim is to publish this volume at a very popular price – if possible at 1/ or 25 cents – and as soon as enough poems have come in to make a record, for today and for tomorrow, of the Negro's struggle for equal rights.
>
> Please send a poem or poems to
>
> Nancy Cunard, <u>Co Lloyds</u>, 43 Boulevard des Capucines, Paris, France[14]

Cunard's tone is undoubtedly odd – who were the intended contributors? One can't help but feel that the shape of her projected revolutionary history ought to have been determined by the revolutionaries themselves. One feels similarly about the strangely pre-determined space of the *Negro* anthology – a detailed analysis and critique of the Scottsboro case (discussed below), and similar cases of racist injustice, is published alongside a highly personal and somewhat predatory essay by the American poet William Carlos Williams about being sexually attracted in his youth to his overly sexualised, permissive black servant girl. It has also been pointed out – justly – that Cunard's self-fetishising image, replete with 'tribal' headgear and jewellery, exceeds the reasonable limits of fashion by purposefully staging photographs in poses that imply victimisation and bondage; when the photographer Barbara Ker Seymer produces a negative photographic print of Cunard, in which her whiteness is turned black, this again seems purposeful and self-annihilating.

Like Alain Locke's *New Negro* published nearly ten years earlier, *Negro* was originally designed as a celebration of black art and literature but soon became an indictment of America's racial divisions, as well as a direct response to the infamous Scottsboro rape case. In 1931, a group of African American boys were falsely accused of raping two white women on a train in Alabama. Speedy trials and death sentences were handed out to the boys, in spite of a clear lack of evidence. The Scottsboro trial quickly became an international symbol of race hatred in the United States, in particular in segregated Southern 'Jim Crow' states. Cunard penned an exhaustive study of the trial, stating that 'the Scottsboro case is not such an astounding and unbelievable thing as it must, as it certainly does, appear to the public at large.' Contrasting it to cases of judicial racism with outwardly political motives, she asserts that 'the same capitalist oppression and brutality are at the root – because every Negro worker is the potential victim of lynching, murder and legal lynching by the white ruling class, simply because he is a worker and black.' Her unrealised *Revolution – the Negro Speaks* seems a likely extension of her efforts for the Scottsboro boys – Cunard, like her friend Kay Boyle, responded to the case in both poetry and journalism. The present volume includes a previously unpublished poem by Cunard entitled 'Rape', for Haywood Patterson, one of the Scottsboro nine. Voiced in the southern dialect of an (imagined?)

white farmer's wife, the poem is chilling and no doubt controversial in its employment of racist language and violence. The poem ends with the words: 'And that was just one more lynching that year / Among the 48 in 1933', suggesting at least a basis in reported fact.

Nancy was disinherited by her mother when she was discovered to be in a relationship with the African American jazz musician Henry Crowder, whom she met in Venice in the summer of 1928. Crowder's band, Eddie South and His Alabamians, were playing at the Luna Hotel, and Nancy was immediately entranced by Crowder's piano skills. She later wrote that Crowder was the first black person she'd ever known, and he became her lover for the next seven years of her life and the source of her interest in producing the *Negro* anthology. This phase of Cunard's life was devoted to the cause of race equality, in particular inequalities suffered by African Americans that Crowder recounted to her, and celebrating the art and culture of the Harlem Renaissance. Cunard and Crowder would travel to Harlem in 1931 and 1932. Cunard was hounded by the American and British press who reported, often erroneously, on her activities in the United States. On more than one occasion she wrote to the international press to clarify, and eventually to seek damages for, falsehoods printed about her company and her title.

In his study of jazz aesthetics and modernism, told through the lives of black Americans Paul Robeson and Josephine Baker, James Donald describes 'jazz modernism' as a 'history of migrations and detours, the movement of ideas and influences as well as of people, between the United States and Europe and back again, as well as across racial borderlines'. Jazz, as music and mode, served as 'symbol and symptom of the modernist attitude'.[15] The importance of Crowder's influence on Cunard's worldview cannot be overstated. In her memoir of the writer Norman Douglas, Cunard recalls meeting Crowder and his band: 'They were Afro-Americans, coloured musicians, and they played in that "out of this world" manner which, in ordinary English, would have to be translated, I suppose, by "ineffable". Such jazz and such Swing and such improvisations! And all new to me in style!'[16] Although Cunard would have been familiar with jazz music before 1928, the 'otherworldly' aspect of Crowder's physical presence, and the band's improvisational live performance of jazz, is remarkable to one who'd spent little actual time around African Americans. Crowder made Cunard aware of the daily racism he and others faced in the United States. In 1930, with Crowder working by her side at the Press, Cunard and he co-produced, a book of poems by Beckett, Aldington, Walter Lowenfels, Harold Acton, and Cunard herself, set to original compositions by Crowder.[17] Both of her poems 'The Boeuf Blues' (inspired by the surrealist ballet *Le Boeuf sur le Toit*) and 'Equatorial Way' are included in this volume. Man Ray's cover for *Henry-Music*, a photograph of Crowder with Cunard's heavily braceleted arms resting on his shoulders, makes for a compelling, suggestive image about their mutual roles.

Cunard's mother used every weapon in her powerful arsenal against her daughter's relationship, including an attempt to legally deport Crowder from England. Nancy described Maud Cunard's racism in embarrassing detail in an eleven-page pamphlet entitled *Black Man and White Ladyship* published in 1931: 'a few days before our going to London last year, what follows had just taken place, and I was unaware of it until our arrival. At a large lunch party in Her Ladyship's house things are set rocking by one of those bombs that throughout her "career" Margot Asquith, Lady Oxford, had been wont to hurl. [...] "Hello, Maud, what is it now – drink, drugs or niggers?" [...] Half of social London is immediately telephoned to: "Is it *true* my daughter knows a Negro?" etc., etc.' Nancy delighted in exposing the conservatism of her mother's aristocratic circle and her own social class. She longed to reject what she felt was their inhumanity, the sickness of their moral hypocrisies.

But Cunard's interest in Africa began long before her meeting with Crowder aged thirty-two. In her memoir of Norman Douglas she recalls:

[at] about six years old, my thoughts began to be drawn toward Africa, and particularly towards the Sahara. Surely I was being taught as much about El Dorado and the North Pole? But there it was: the Desert. The sand, the dunes, the huge spaces, mirages, heat and parchedness – I seemed able to visualize all of this. Of

such were filled several dreams, culminating in the great night-
mare in which I wandered, repeatedly, the whole of one agonising
night, escaping through a series of tents somewhere in the Sahara.
Later came extraordinary dreams about black Africa – 'The Dark
Continent' – with Africans dancing and drumming around me,
and I one of them, though still white, knowing, mysteriously
enough, how to dance in their own manner. Everything was full of
movement in these dreams; it was that which enabled me to escape
in the end, going further, even further! And all of it was a mixture
of apprehension that sometimes turned into joy, and even rapture.

Initially, Cunard's dreamed-up African landscape is unpeopled, a
sea of sand and endlessly iterative undulating space. The introduc-
tion of time (an 'agonising night') and figures of Africans dancing
and drumming, turns an inescapable nightmare into a liberating,
almost anonymising rhythm. There is intense satisfaction grounded
in communal movement and the deferral of recognition or self-con-
sciousness. To an extent Cunard's biographers and critics, such as
Jane Marcus and Maroula Joannou, read her wish for exoticism
and identification with the racial 'Other' as an expression of her
wish to escape her socially privileged (and thereby repugnant) self.
For Nancy, Africa was an idea rather than an actual place – her
mother's connections at the British consulate barred her from trav-
elling farther south than the Maghreb. Without a doubt, Henry
Crowder was Cunard's doorway into black culture. He gave her
access to other black intellectuals and artists, and enabled her to be
a legitimate advocate for civil rights and anti-imperialist, anti-na-
tionalist movements. Crowder remembers in his memoir that
Cunard repeatedly exhorted him to 'Be more African!', to which he
replied 'I'm not African, I'm American', much to her displeasure.[18]
Needless to say, if Nancy was masquerading as oppressed then she
was keen on casting those around her in the appropriate supporting
roles. In the most direct terms, one cannot deny that Cunard's
fantasy of otherness plays itself out in a radicalised political order
that relies on her authority as enforcer of such values. Consider her
poem 'Psalm for Trinidad', the first in a short pamphlet published
in 1941 in Havana titled *Psalm of the Palms*:

Psalm for Trinidad

I am Trinidad – Columbus discovered me,
Land of the Carib then, land of palm-trees, humming-birds,
I am Africa, India now; gone are slaves and indentured labour,
The songs of these am I, the wage-serfs, under a still-Victorian
                                                    Union Jack.

  (*Oh de sun de sun ha laash me; it 96 in de shade.*)
[...]
I am the cane-break, the largest sugar-factory in the Empire,
Thin silent folk of India in those fields, dividends, engineers,
Bullock-carts, piety – brown hands splitting the golden
cocoa-pods,
African faces in green depths, silent too, wondering 'how long dis
                                                    way?'

  (*40 cents, 20 cents – depend if I am man or woman – it so, my day.*)
[...]
I am Calypso, brown bards of the people improvising irony in
                                                    song;
I am the multitude, the articulate, keen
Brown face and black and gold; the courteous Chinese
Trading in towns, Indians passing mute almost ghostly;
I am the young hotheads, the cackle of old dark laughter, the ripe
                                    vernacular on the roads...

  (*What about after de war, man you think it come to Democracy?*)
[...]
I am the Iron Music, the fork on the bottle with the spoon,
The drum out of Africa, the tambu-bambu, the collective Carnival;
Always always a note of sadness under the singing,
Always a wistfulness, an uncertainty, a back-bringing...
[...]
Trinidad, effervescent -------
                    look at me, look at me, look at me here.

In a way this is not so far from the monolithic otherness of Cunard's childhood dream – even the 'courteous Chinese' are passive, but for song – reminding us of Whitman's 'wage labourer as Democratic America' portraits and the all-encompassing lyrical self that silences by singing. The final lines of the poem, 'Trinidad, effervescent ------ / look at me, look at me, look at me here', are strangely ambiguous; the position of the subject is unclear, or rather, the multiple voices of blackness and oppression result in a displacement of the lyrical 'I' by the plurality of 'me'. The final poem in *Psalm of the Palms*, titled 'In answer to Trinidad's poet who asks me "...What was it moved you to enlist / In our sad cause your all of heart and soul?"' and dedicated to Alfred Cruickshank, offers an additional clue.

> My friend, ship rocks, and seas come great and small
> Over the gunwale, but the captain reads
> On, despite this. On land the teeming seeds
> Breed without fear, and after the gusty fall
> Of rain comes ready are they, present, erect,
> Grown. Do you sense the symbol in it all?
> The man outlives the storm, the tribunal
> Of nature judges, tempering the elect.
> Our lives are wars – You ask: 'Why love the slave,
> The "noble savage" in the planter's grave,
> And us, descendants in a hostile clime?'
> Call of the conscious sphere, I, nature and man,
> Answer you: 'Brother, instinct, knowledge... and then
> Maybe I was an African one time.'

Cunard lamented that she did not have any actual African blood (instead she insisted that she had the soul of an African), but her levelling of insurmountable class and racial boundaries in the natural world of Trinidad (surrounded by sea and plagued by the labour of agriculture) is eye-wateringly direct. As a self-appointed conduit between black and white culture and society, Cunard's work is defined by this kind of reciprocity (idealistic and naive though it may be). Her willingness and ability to mimic the rootlessness and alienation of historically displaced people is fascinating both in and of itself, but also as a document of modernity more generally. After her relationship with Crowder deteriorated and the *Negro* anthology failed to garner press attention, Cunard headed south to report on the war in Spain.

In 1937, near the start of the Spanish Civil War, Cunard distributed a questionnaire among writers and poets: 'Are you for, or against, the legal Government and the People of Republican Spain? Are you for, or against, Franco and Fascism?' Cunard, along with W. H. Auden, Louis Aragon, Pablo Neruda, and Stephen Spender, signed their names to the charge against Fascism: 'For it is impossible any longer to take no side.' Among the many printed responses are several notable writers who support the left-wing communist government democratically elected in 1936, including Kay Boyle, Rebecca West, Ford Madox Ford, Aldous Huxley, C. Day Lewis, C. L. R. James, and Leonard Woolf. The poet David Gascoyne writes: 'One would have to be devoid of the most elementary feelings for decency and justice in order to preserve an attitude of indifference towards the inhuman gangster warfare being waged by Fascism against the people of Spain and their elected government.'[19] A handful of neutral replies – and a smaller handful of responses favouring Fascism (Evelyn Waugh, Edmund Blunden) – are equally intriguing in view of Britain's neutrality. Eliot, who also refused to contribute to *Negro*, writes: 'While I am naturally sympathetic, I still feel convinced that it is best that at least a few men of letters should remain isolated, and take no part in these collective activities.' Perhaps Ezra Pound's reply is most fascinating of all those Cunard included: 'Questionnaire an escape mechanism for young fools who are too cowardly to think; to lazy to investigate the nature of money, its mode of issue, the control of such an issue by the Banque de France and the stank of England. You are all had. Spain is an emotional luxury to a gang of sap-headed dilettantes.'[20] At this point Pound was living in Italy and had expressed support for Mussolini's fascist government. His conspiracies about banking and usury notwithstanding, Pound's objections and Eliot's unwillingness to take sides on the grounds of intellectual freedom must have been disappointing to Cunard. Nevertheless, all three thousand copies of *Authors Take Sides on the*

Spanish War sold out, with proceeds going to the Spanish cause.

According to Lois Gordon, Cunard's most recent biographer, Cunard spent much of the war as a journalist for various newspapers, first arriving into Barcelona in August 1936. Her despatches from the Front found their way into her poetry during this period, sometimes taking on the reportage quality of her eye-witness accounts for the *Manchester Guardian*. Her 1938 poem, 'To Eat Today', written during the bombardment of Barcelona, begins with an epigraph from 'the press': 'In Barcelona today's air raid came as we were sitting down to lunch after reading Hitler's speech in Nüremberg.'

> You heroes of Nazi stamp, you sirs in the ether,
> Sons of Romulus, Wotan – is the mark worth the bomb?
> What was in it? salt, and a half-pint of olive,
> Nothing else but the woman, she treasured it terribly,
> Oil for the day folks would come, refugees from Levante,
> Maybe with greens... one round meal... but you killed her,
> Killed four children outside, with the house, and the pregnant cat.
> Hail, hand of Rome, you passed – and that is all.

Cunard details the cruelty of the indiscriminate aerial bombing of civilians. Spain, and her experiences witnessing bombing campaigns by Franco's forces and its allies as well as the exodus of starving refugees fleeing into relocation camps in France from Catalonia, never left Cunard's imagination. Well into the last years of her life, she continued to work on her unfinished 'Epic on Spain', which included her observations from return visits in the 1950s and early 1960s. In a section omitted from the manuscript of her 'Epic' held at Oxford University's Bodleian Library, but restored in the present volume, Cunard writes:

> I cannot compute the bodies, cannot compass the dead.
> And one day
> Came from the sky this, a present to the earth:
> Journalist's despatch, November something: "Witnessed today
> opening of box dropped over Madrid by parachute of Francoist

plane. Contents, horribly mutilated body. Carved-up corpse of
Republican aviator. Obviously work of professional butcher. Note
attached: 'We will serve all your fliers in like manner.'"

His name was Juan Antonio Galarza.[21]

Her 'Epic' – and all the poems she wrote from Spain during the
war – are polyvocal and polylinguistic (she was fluent in both
Spanish and Catalan) and incorporate local languages and voices
in ways that are colloquial and intimate. The poem's act of witness,
grounded in Cunard's textual strategies that place the sufferer at
the heart of her writing, is poignant. Never does her own strong
political will upstage real, lived experience. Her bravery as a jour-
nalist, poet, and advocate for the many refugees (both civilian and
military) housed by Vichy France in Perpignan in 'reception centres'
that amounted to concentration camps is a part of Cunard's wider,
tireless campaign against the spread of fascist powers throughout
Europe and North Africa (indeed, at one point she was able to
rescue five prisoners – including the poet César Arconada – and
take them to her house in Réanville).[22]

In 1937, the year of her *Authors Take Sides*, Cunard raised funds
for the Spanish resistance through another publication, this time
hand-printed by her at the Hours Press, with Neruda's assistance.
Six pamphlets of poetry were produced entitled *The Poets of the
World Defend the Spanish People!* These pamphlets included poems
by Tristan Tzara, the executed Andalusian poet Federico Garcia-
Lorca, Langston Hughes, Raphael Alberti, and W. H. Auden (his
now well-known poem 'Spain'), among others. With the Scotts-
boro trial, Cunard's advocacy for black Americans in the United
States (and, by extension, the black Atlantic) had roused her sense
of injustice in otherwise democratic societies. The rise of Fascism
in Europe during the Spanish Civil War and into the Second
World War crucially inspired her distrust of nationalism, patri-
otism and, most acutely, political apathy.

Among Cunard's archived manuscripts from the 1930s is a
poem dedicated to the controversial social Darwinist and eugen-
icist Bernelot Moens, who theorised classifications of humanity

through the ages into 'primitive', 'civilised', 'humanised', 'cultured' and, finally, 'perfect' man. The perfect man was a future condition of society, one in which all race hatred and prejudice – and indeed, borders – would no longer exist. The perfect man emerges from 'the world in fusion', total racial mixing, and hence heralds an end to discrimination.

> The Supra-Nation crests the racial seas,
> Docks in new sunset splendours, where the great
> Banquet transcendent science that no State
> May triumph over. Yet, my friend, what frees
> The peon's hands that raised the warrior's shield,
> The loin-clothed coolie in the paddy-field?

> (from 'To Professor Bernelot Moens')

Written in 1934, the year the *Negro* anthology was published, Cunard's celebration of an anti-nation on a cruise ship is revealing. The urge to eradicate boundaries of class, race and nationality – again mediated through the sea, a space of forced forgetting – may just be an inexact desire for self-determination, played through the terrible rejection of whiteness, Americanness, Englishness, wealth, and privilege – all categories to which Cunard was 'guilty' of belonging. Cunard's archive is full of photographs of African artefacts – masks, statues, and of course jewellery. Surveying these, one senses her careful scholarly dedication as she handles and surrounds herself with the living objects of her dreams. At best, Cunard's activism was a wish for a community – preferably for a community of outsiders, of others like herself, for whom she could reject her wealth, her class, and the privileges of her name.

After the devastating psychological blow of losing her home in Réanville after it was pillaged by German troops and French locals, followed by the death of her (still estranged) mother in 1948, Cunard returned to London. She spent much of the following years travelling through France and Spain (both dramatically changed since the wars) as well as Chile (invited by her close friend Neruda), the West Indies, and Cuba. There is evidence to suggest that Cunard was involved with the exiled Spanish Maquis and their continuing covert resistance against Franco's regime by helping soldiers and their families escape, and that she even took lessons in dynamiting.[23] Cunard's poem 'Relève into Maquis', published by the small Derby-based Grasshopper Press in 1944, is a criticism of Vichy France's 'relève', or exchange policy, that traded skilled workers with Nazi Germany for French prisoners of war from 1942 onwards. Using the language of French prime minister Pierre Laval's government propaganda, Cunard undercuts the lies therein and the relève's implicit collaboration with other forms of enforced deportation. She also glorifies the Maquis and their covert attempts to undermine fascist rule in France, Germany, and Spain. The poem's anonymous heroic fighter, a veteran of Spain, is 'Enlisted until war's end – / Not to see folks or friends again – Don't count on any pay – / Death if your weapon's lost – Total secrecy, death if not –'. 'Relève into Maquis' is a rousing battle cry that ends with the words 'signed, FRANCE.' In 1943 and 1944 Cunard collected and published (through La France Libre and Pierre Seghers) seventy *Poems for France*, a celebration of the resistance movement that was published both in French and English. One astonishingly didactic poem Cunard wrote in 1944, 'Man–Ship–Tank–Gun–Plane' stands out – not just for its title's Futurist syntax, but for its sweeping head-on depiction of battle, reminiscent of poems by F. T. Marinetti or Blaise Cendrars, only with a great deal more humility and, indeed, humanity.

During the early 1940s, Cunard wrote and planned an unfinished series of seven poems for seven countries called 'Passport to Freedom', a bold transnational pamphlet written in Spanish, Italian, French, and English. Her seventh country, the United States, the country of her mother's birth, remained unwritten; by her own admission she got no further than the line 'Up from the grassy roots'.[24] A partial typescript for this exists in Cunard's archive, dated spring 1942, and three of the poems were published in newspapers, including *The New Statesman*. Not quite the cruising 'Supra-Nation', this series of poems accounted for boundaries but moved freely across them – a privilege Cunard did not always enjoy when faced with borders enforced by war. Taken together, they make a compelling case for transnational modernism and the internationalism of Cunard's literary and political allegiances.

Traces of other planned collections can be found in Cunard's archived manuscripts, including her aforementioned 'Epic on Spain' and two unrealised larger projects, 'The Visions' (or 'Cosmo's Dream') and a collection of poems now referred to as the Bodleian Manuscript, or Augustan Manuscript, completed in 1944. Cunard focused her energies on several literary works during the 1950s including her book-length 'memories' of the writers George Moore and Norman Douglas, two figures who had occupied fatherly roles during her early life. She also produced a book of poems in French about Spain written between 1945–49, *Nous Gens d'Espagne* (We People of Spain). A combination of a mental breakdown in 1960, respiratory complaints from life-long smoking and drinking, and a series of falls which resulted in a broken hip, meant that Cunard spent much of 1963 bedridden, after periods in both London's St Clement's Hospital and Holloway Sanatorium at Virginia Water in 1960. Her copious notebooks and journals – dutifully recording the name of the café or far-flung city in which she is writing – become more and more feverish and difficult to decipher from 1960 onwards. Although her poems written in Holloway Sanatorium are neatly handwritten (often at a window or in the communal TV room, taking stock of hospital rituals and members of staff), they are not reproduced in this volume. However, their titles are enough to gauge their contents: 'Sonnet for Jock-the-Scot (Jock Duff of the L.C.C.)'; 'Mistresses Perjury and Collusion on the Magistrate's Knee (Café Holloway Jail April 6 1960 N–11,582 (ME–NC)'; 'To Nurse Phillips' (written in eight minutes); 'I, Scarlet Broad'; '2 sonnets written while Geoffrey Horam made a coloured crayon portrait of me 10–11 AM 1960 June 28'. Perhaps one ought to be mindful of Cunard's 1963 poem 'The Artist to Himself', hand-written in a notebook whilst staying with friends at Villa Pomone in Saint-Jean-Cap-Ferrat. In it she warns,

Never show unfinished work!
No one will understand.

'Spontaneous ravings of the mind'...
Not even best friends at hand.
The way to deal with things of that kind
Is work and work and work
Upon the poem, music, stone
That's yours, and only yours alone,
Until its very end.

Then show it all, without a word,
To others; that pleasing shout
(if any!) of praise may then be heard
(Not that that will remove thy doubt
As to the valour of the thing;
Yet still, some solace bring...)
Enfevered creation, it is good
But only with *patience* in the blood
Itself of the very thing.

Cunard dates the start of her long poem 'The Visions' to 1964, during her painful convalescence post-hip surgery in Pomone,[25] but her biographer dates the composition somewhat earlier. The poem is incomplete in both typescript and notebook drafts. Cunard's introduction to two sequences from the poem reads as follows.

The theme of it all, roughly, this: Cosmo, the poet, who appears later in this early part which is entirely about the Medieval Halls and the singers there, leaves one night in a rage, finds himself, the next day (one may suppose this is all between the years 1000 and 1200 AD) with some of the visions of that great Castle which he has left on his horse, Mead, and sleeps the night in the hay of their barn, while on his way who knows whither. At first, and at once, surges a long dream, and it is all about Fish, and only about Fish. The dream itself merges into the first of the Visions proper, and this, by chance, is simply Adam. After this comes many and very various visions, culminating in our age of 'nuclear fission', when Cosmo may be said to issue from them.

Wagner's *Tristan and Isolde*, Swinburne and various other figures from history and literature appear central to this dream-vision and the role of the poet as unifier of time and human history. It is an ambitious if bewildering work that, in its breadth and learning (obscure, sometimes archaic references to art and literature) warrants further study.

The only Selection of Cunard's poems that predates the present one is a reproduction of a 1944 typescript housed in the Edward John Thompson Papers at the Bodleian Library, published by Nottingham Trent Editions as *The Poems of Nancy Cunard: From the Bodleian Library* in 2005, edited and introduced by John Lucas. Thompson was a writer, historian of India and translator of Rabindranath Tagore whose political sympathies (gradually becoming in favour of Indian self-government) would have chimed with Cunard's. Thompson's archive contains several letters and poems which he and Cunard were deliberating over, including some destined for a collection in his 'Augustan Modern Poets' series, published by Ernest Benn. Cunard was enthusiastic about the project, mostly because of her respect for Thompson and because the books were cheaply priced (at 9d) and therefore accessible to a wider audience. Her delight at the price, and her own knowledge of the book market, may even be part of the reason that she had shunned mainstream book-length publishing after her second collection in 1923. For whatever reason, Cunard's Bodleian/Augustan manuscript languished after Thompson's unexpected illness and death in April 1946 from stomach cancer, and she did not pursue it. Cunard did, however, dedicate her 'Man–Ship–Tank–Gun–Plane' to Thompson, a fellow political radical.[26] By Cunard's own admission it is a scant selection, omitting many of her poems from *Outlaws* and *Sublunary*. Judging by their correspondence, Cunard realised how different her first two books were from the material she later produced during three major wars. She was keen to disown her earlier work, that which was written before her 'social consciousness time' (1926–28).[27] In a letter to Thompson on 10 December 1943 she writes:

Here are some more poems. I have had a dreadful three days going through Wheels, Outlaws and Sublunary, copying the entire lot, once and for all, of these O.O.P.s. They are quite terrible, quite terrible these books, and I can't think how they got printed. There is NOTHING else that I could bear you to look at in those three books. You'll see however, that I have extracted a very few, and these I think can pass. Parallax too I am greatly dismayed at, most of it, but these two sequences can pass. I think *I begin to write a poem* with Simultaneous and In Provins; only from then on.

Thompson was clearly keen to offer a balanced and representative view of Cunard's poetic oeuvre, but she fiercely resisted reprinting more than three poems written before 1925, feeling that they were badly written and immature. She also claims that between roughly 1926 and 1936 she wrote almost no poems at all.[28] Finally, Thompson relents when Cunard insists 'They are downright bad, or at least very inferior, and I will NOT be represented by them. I will *NOT*.'[29] By 1945, Cunard had returned to Réanville to face the devastation of her once home and what remained of the Hours Press. Thompson appears to have passed the task of editing Cunard's manuscript to someone else during his illness. Although Cunard mentions that she is planning a large edition of her later poems, to be entitled *The Lands That Were Today* after her poem for Kay Boyle, neither book appeared and Cunard went back to publishing small pamphlets, often at her own expense.

Notwithstanding Cunard's disavowal of her early poetry, the value of her modernist poem *Parallax* as a whole is indisputable, as is, I would argue, the value of her several World War 1 and European travel poems from *Outlaws* and *Sublunary*. Here are the seeds of her political consciousness, her rejection of British nationalism in favour of internationalism, and her early aesthetic forays into modernist avant-garde poetics. Cunard's near-entire poetic output, viewed as a whole, provides a different sort of picture of the poet, one that charts the hope and despair of her generation and reflects the best of its artistic aims.

A recent reprint of *The Poets of the World Defend the Spanish People!* includes a recollection by Ramón J. Sender of Cunard's passion for art as a means towards social justice: 'Nancy Cunard was a bold heroine of the battle against the inexpressible. The inexpressible that, as we say, waits and needs to be expressed.'[30] Writing about her in the late 1920s, the poet and artist Mina Loy vividly captures her friend's spiritual and visual alterity, as well as her fragile form, in her poem 'Nancy Cunard'. What Loy could not have envisioned here is the tremendous strength and unflinching idealism of Cunard's literary legacy.

> Your eyes diffused with holly lights
> of ancient Christmas
> helmeted with masks
> whose silken nostrils
> point the cardinal airs,
>
> The vermilion wall
> receding as a sin
> beyond your moonstone whiteness,
>
> Your chiffon voice
> tears with soft mystery
> a lily loaded with a sucrose dew
> of vigil carnival,
>
> Your lone fragility
> of mythological queens
> conjures long-vanished dragons –
> – their vast jaws
> yawning in disillusion,
>
> Your drifting hands
> faint as exotic snow
> spread silver silence
>
> as a fondant nun
> framed in the facing profiles
> of Princess Murat
> and George Moore.[31]

NOTES

1 Mulk Raj Anand, *Conversations in Bloomsbury* (London: Wildwood House, 1981), pp. 37–39.

2 Nancy Cunard, *These Were the Hours: Memoires of My Hours Press*, ed. Hugh Ford (Carbondale: Southern Ilinois University Press, 1969), pp. 201–204.

3 Lois Gordon, *Nancy Cunard: Heiress, Muse, Political Idealist* (New York: Columbia University Press, 2007), p. 25.

4 Denis Donoghue, *Irish Essays* (Cambridge: Cambridge University Press, 2011), p. 79.

5 Nancy Cunard, letter to John Hayward, 11 January 1965, The Papers of John Davy Hayward, Kings College Archive Centre, Cambridge.

6 T. S. Eliot, *The Waste Land: A facsimile and transcript of the original drafts*, ed. Valerie Eliot (London: Faber and Faber, 1971), p. 27.

7 Gordon, pp. 62–64.

8 Nancy Cunard, letter to Ezra Pound, 11 June 1946, Nancy Cunard Papers, Harry Ransom Center (Texas), box 10, folder 6.

9 Gordon, pp. 99–106.

10 Cunard, *These Were the Hours*, p. 8.

11 Gordon, p. 122.

12 Jane Dowson, *Women, Modernism and British Poetry, 1910–1939: Resisting Femininity* (Aldershot: Ashgate, 2002), p. 117. Dowson's book also provides an excellent contextualization of women poets involved in the Spanish Civil War, including Sylvia Townsend Warner and Valentine Ackland, both friends of Cunard's.

13 Cunard, *These Were the Hours*, p. 7.

14 Nancy Cunard Papers, Harry Ransom Center, box 8, folder 6.

15 James Donald, *Some of These Days: Black Stars, Jazz Aesthetics, and Modernist Culture* (Oxford: Oxford University Press, 2015), pp. 18–19.

16 As quoted in Anthony Barnett, *Listening for Henry Crowder: A Monograph on His Almost Lost Music* (Lewes: Allardyce, Barnett, Publishers, 2007), pp. 20–21. Barnett's book offers a vivid account of Cunard's impressions.

17 For more on Crowder's life and music see *As Wonderful as All That? Henry Crowder's Memoir of His Affair with Nancy Cunard, 1928–1935* (Navarro, California: Wild Trees Press, 1987) and Barnett's excellent *Listening for Henry Crowder*.

18 Gordon, p. 180.

19 *Authors Take Sides on the Spanish War* (first published by *Left Review*, 1937. Reissued by Cecil Woolf Publishers, London, 2001), p. 14.

20 Ibid. p. 32.

21 Nancy Cunard Papers, Harry Ransom Center, box 7, folder 3.

22 Gordon, p. 259.

23 Gordon, p. 311.

24 Nancy Cunard Papers, Harry Ransom Center, box 7, folder 6.

25 Nancy Cunard Papers, Harry Ransom Center, box 8, folder 4.

26 John Lucas, introduction to *Poems of Nancy Cunard: From the Bodleian Library* (Nottingham, Trent Editions, 2005), p. 18.

27 Letter from Nancy Cunard to Edward Thompson, 29 Feb 1943, Edward John Thompson Papers, University of Oxford, Bodleian Library, MS Eng c. 5285.

28 Letter from NC to ET, 23 Feb 1944, ibid.

29 Letter from NC to ET, 29 Feb 1943, ibid.

30 *Los Poetas del Mundo Defendian al Pueblo Español*, ed. Pablo Neruda and Nancy Cunard (Spanish reprint, Sevilla: Renacimiento, 2010), p. 79.

31 Mina Loy, *The Lost Lunar Baedeker*, ed. Roger Conover (Manchester: Carcanet Press, 1997), p. 103.

Outlaws

1921

Outlaws

I

There is a curious legend of two lovers
That thrills within the heart of every man;
Ghostly they are, yet living, and the span
Allotted them by fate no end discovers.
There was a man, adventurous and free,
Evil of soul, grown into league with hell,
Loved by a woman that no fear might quell;
Their lives rose as the waves grow out at sea.
Wild as the glory of a desert lion,
Dark as the sombre magnitude of death,
Heavy with memories as a storm that saith
Aloud its toll of corpses... Cruel iron
Lay as a heart within this man, yet still
She followed him; he held her to his will.

II

Her heart held many musics; many songs
Shone like fair crystals in her tenderness,
And all her longing was for happiness;
Yet love was darkened by her lover's wrongs
And wild unlawful piracies, though he
Worshipped with passion, elemental flame
That burns, consuming self; the soul untame
Burnt in each freely. They shall never see
The shuddering brinks behind them, never know
The perilous moments nor the cruel hour
When death strove for them; but with haunted eyes
Speed to infinity, while all this slow
World's musing chronicle records the power
That dwelt in their strange love that never dies.

III

And so they wandered through life's haunted rooms,
Each other's heart laid bare to each, and hid
In secrecy from all the rest, amid
Their happiness and tragedies and glooms.
Life drew its ghosts around them, and on walls
Lingered strange shadows that were more than life
In their deep artifice. A trenchant knife
Above them hung, the knife that never falls
But trembles in its warning. Voices came
From out the elements, from sea and fire
To lead them on; they conquered all desire
With passion ever-new. Adventure's flame
Was sealed upon their souls that did aspire
And reached up to the transient face of fame.

IV

Outlawed, aloof, like thunderclouds they sped
Over the restless breathing of the sea;
And those around shook at their liberty,
And trembled at their power. Alone the dead
Were free from these magicians' modern charms
That vaunted lawlessness and love and pleasure:
Drawing the brave into a swifter measure,
Leading the brave into the life that harms
All but its strange initiate. Their crimes
Sped down the course of nature unrestrained.
While others fell they conquered, careful, trained,
Well practised in their art; yet there were times
Most near to death – then she, who loved so well,
Saved him, and straightway gave her soul to hell.

V

Love was too little for him, fate too strong,
And took in payment from him folly's toll;
And yet she loved him with a patience long,
And eyes kept clear wherewith to view the soul,
The shaking battlefield that nourished him
And filled with tempests the proud tortured eyes
That mirrored her reflected love, yet grim,
Brooding remained; as by a fire that dies
Sits an impenitent with ravenous crimes
That will not cry aloud nor mercy seek,
Through haunted midnights sped with cruel chimes,
Locked in himself – till finally the sleek
Pale face of morning puts to flight the dim,
Mad, raving, windy ghosts that follow him.

VI

Flayed souls that flee before a shivering wind
Out to the dark horizons of the sea;
Eternal wanderers that may never be
Stilled by the touch of death. A pirate's mind
Steers their black ships; his soul makes full their sails
With the wild winds of courage, and the waves
Daily grow great between them over graves
Of others not so free. When daylight fails
They may be seen alongside each to each,
Two lovers passionate of life and stress,
Stepped from the lands of hell to earth above:
A man that failed with heaven in his reach,
And she, that should have crowned a king, no less,
Yet then as now held but her crown of love.

VII

One thinks to hear them crying in the wind:
'Life was so bitter to us – but we chose
The living, stressful moments from this close
Denying, grey existence. If we sinned
We bear our joys and crimes with equal heart,
And punishment is nothing. We have known
All sweet and sharp adventures, and are grown
Heroic-hard with life. You cannot part
Our twin minds from each other, and we sail
Proud and forever on the clutching sea,
Grown element again; the heaven's breath
Makes clear our souls with space; life does not fail
As we have used it.'... They shall ever be;
Summer has set upon them but not death.

And if the End Be Now?...

The rooms are empty and the streets are bare,
No lovers meet at midnight under stars,
And the past pleasures of congenial hours
Forgotten lie; yet now these flowers that fade
Once dressed the gardens with gay delight.
Ah, patiently we must grow friends with grey,
Put out of mind the colour of the flame
And the triumphant songs of inspiration;
Obliterate adventure, memory.
The silence of desertion has begun
And the slow madness of annihilation;
Think you we can be friends with nothingness
And make a song out of an empty hour?
Somewhere the world has changed, the sun slipped round
To lands antipodean, leaving us

Like wandering dreamers in long corridors
That may not be got through, a circular maze
That guards the promised land of Never More;
Alone, alone we wander with our dream –
Ah, I have felt remote before tonight,
As if some word had drifted down from God
To warn my soul of the eventual end
And the completed solitude to be.
I have felt married to eternity,
Already bade farewell to things and days,
And seen their transmutation into ghosts
That gravely intimate the parting sign –
And if the end be now have I known all?
Let us examine conscience' hieroglyph...
The adolescent love of mysticism,
Followed by bitter sceptic pride and scorn
Of what life seemed to give, gave into hands
Too frail to hold, looked into eyes too veiled
With youthful sorrows to let comfort in.
And there was independence, solemnly
Scheming to build the tower impregnable
That should throw shadow over half the earth;
And fortitude and courage, like wild steeds
They raved and never could be brought to rein,
And so made havoc, vainly wasting strength
Till their nobility was lost indeed.
Love came along and seemed the conqueror
That should set right the world, proclaiming justice
With many promises of inspiration
And a high creed of generosity;
(Of all religions Love the proudest is,
And will not be gainsaid, but though eternal,
By its own flame it fades, consuming us).
There have been other martyrs on this wheel
That turns today before me: introspection,
And that fanatic, self-analysis,
With soul archaic as the early saint

That knelt with grace to clasp the cross and death;
But oh, my saint dies not! and glories still
Turning the knife each day in painful wounds
With self-infliction growing ever deeper...
Yet there are moods when I can plumb the world
And seem to tell the purpose of the stars,
Grasp at the palm of fate, transcending earth.
This is the tranquil mood of certainty
That lies above us as the distant sunset.

*   *   *   *   *   *

After the beat of sorrow's passionate hands
Came melancholy with a gesture calm;
And in her motion was the breath of sleep
And musing poetry, to soothe despair;
And here time seemed to turn a gentle hermit
Putting aside the weary web of stress;
Akin with nature, merging into autumn
With a long pause as if eternal – Then
The human world obtrudes, the daily tides
Of feverish events surge up again
And to a further controversy beckon.

*   *   *   *   *   *

My hands are empty now, my heart as void
Of all emotions as a timeless dawn
When the last stars are lost, before some day
Has made complete actuality of hours.
Now close the doors and let the pulse of earth
Slip unperceived to final quietude,
For life has taken much in giving much –
In that shall lie the balance of the end.

Moon

Slowly the moon grows larger, I can see
The real solitude to be tonight,
And the vain longing of a muted heart
As when two lovers have been long asunder.
She counts the minutes, pale and silently
Draws nearer to the sea; the little waves
Become all great with longing, wreath'd with foam;
Already a long stairway from the sky
Descending slowly rests upon the earth,
And thoughts, like spirits, on it come and go.

*   *   *   *   *   *

Oh puissant unattainable white moon,
My soul has taken pause, saluting thee.

The Sonnet of Happiness

Over the City lie the gathered stars,
The streets are holy in their emptiness
As I go with you, great with happiness.
We have inherited the strength of Mars
And the proud love of Venus; we are free!
Let us make good our freedom, for we are wise
And bravely passionate; this enterprise
Shall long endure like a fine ship at sea.
Tonight we'll have no melodrama, tears,
Or sudden partings of dissatisfaction,
No wavering purpose or unglorious action,
No hesitation or uncertain fears;
But in a solitude of silence Grecian
Shall know the plenitude of life's completion.

I

[What is this cry for toys? you've had them all]

What is this cry for toys? you've had them all;
This clamouring for lovers? take your choice:
Outgrown and senseless dolls with timid voice,
Like marionettes unstrung they can but fall
Into your merciful hands, your tender grasp
That pities them and tidies up their tears;
The while you wince, yet put away their fears,
Their sorrows soothe, their anguished hands un-clasp.
For they have sunk all pride in commonness,
Lost the contumely look, the daily speech;
Lie at your feet – bend down, let fingers reach
An ultimate kiss to them – forgetfulness…
And then maybe your sorrows, each by each,
Will pardon beg for you, end your distress.

II

[Yet when the night draws on, you long for arms]

Yet when the night draws on, you long for arms,
Arms to enfold, becalm your soul away,
Gestures to quell, a voice that says: 'Today
Is a spent nightmare, rest you from alarms
And be unharassed; you have done with fear
For a short season and shall claim reward,
That share of victory that has been stored
For you in well-kept sequence, costing dear.'
And in the sunset stillness of that hour
Maybe you'll dream of lying down with Death,
Your ultimate lover; but your soul and breath

Must first be parted by that unknown power
Of time or fate, whatever name is given
To that strange path that's said to lead to heaven.

Praise

I love the gesture of your open hands
Expounding things: the blinding streak of fire
That lights the voice of your imagination.
I love your laugh and all its cadences,
The tempests of your speech, the flaming words
Of wisdom, all the agile nimble thoughts
That seethe and simmer in your smiling brain;
The oratory of truths you have declaimed,
The conquest of the difficult and dark
Obstructions laid by life along your way.
You have not fallen, failed nor faltered once,
Nor looked behind in doubt, but undismayed
Have faced the sun. In your dark eyes I see
The promises of miracles, the lure
Of brilliant new horizons, hopes found good,
And dreams to make the gods rejoice and sing.

You are an army flushed with conquered wines,
Feasting on luxury and new delight –
You are the king of joy, the world is tamed
And spread before you in magnificence;
The subtle and the sensuous are your slaves,
And all the seven wonders now made clear
Delivered you as prize. I will stand by
And look into a corner of your heart
To see if you are happy, if your crown
Be not of gold too heavy, whether pain
Shall be excluded from this great new rule,

And all the sorrows and incertitudes
Put to the torture they have merited.
I think that you will now make free our days,
And conquer time; you shall not know defeat.

For you are priest of Possibility,
Hero of new-discovered continents,
Pure as the endless sea, spirit of love
Created from the essences of stars
And the pulsating powers of elements;
There are no bounds nor limits to your speed,
No mountain huge enough to crush your heart,
Nothing to kill the genius of your soul.

The Lovers

Hundreds of lovers there have been,
        Princes and clowns and fools;
Mighty, timid, low, obscene,
And some whose hearts were never clean
        Who set aside all rules.

Dark lovers from the burning lands,
        And giants from the plain,
And some with wicked cruel hands,
And some God made and understands,
        And more that Death has slain.

Pale boys too beautiful to live,
        Too wild and proud and young,
With eager eyes and hearts that give
A love this life cannot forgive
        And sends its snakes among.

And some that lied and stole and swore
    To fill the world with vice,
Who fought each other and made war
Till Fate came knocking at the door
    And made them pay the price.

Strange subtlety, sweet happiness
    Some gave and others took!
Yet lovers all, who once did bless
The love that leads men to distress
    And marks with bitter look.

Now Death has stolen all away,
    And bade them love and kiss
Pale shadows of a yesterday,
With empty hands and hearts that sway
    In darker worlds than this.

Wheels

I sometimes think that all our thoughts are wheels,
Rolling forever through a painted world:
Moved by the cunning of a thousand clowns
Dressed paper-wise, with blatant rounded masks,
That take their multi-coloured caravans
From place to place, and act and leap and sing,
Catching the spinning hoops when cymbals clash.
And one is dressed as Fate, and one as Death;
The rest that represent Love, Joy and Sin,
Join hands in solemn stage-learnt ecstasy,
While Folly beats a drum with golden pegs,
And mocks that shrouded jester called Despair.
The dwarfs and other curious satellites,
Voluptuous-mouthed, with slyly pointed steps

Strut in the circus while the people stare.
And some have sober faces white with chalk
And roll the heavy wheels all through the streets
Of sleeping hearts, with ponderance and noise
Like weary armies on a solemn march.
Now in the scented gardens of the Night
Where we are scattered like a pack of cards,
Our words are turned to spokes that thoughts may roll,
And form a ringing chain around the world,
(Itself a fabulous wheel controlled by Time
Over the slow incline of centuries).
So dreams and prayers, and feelings born of sleep,
As well as all the sun-gilt pageantry
Made out of summer breezes and hot noons,
Are in the great revolving of the spheres
Under the trampling of their chariot wheels.

Zeppelins

I saw the people climbing up the street
Maddened with war and strength and thought to kill;
And after followed Death, who held with skill
His torn rags royally, and stamped his feet.

The fires flamed up and burnt the serried town,
Most where the sadder, poorer houses were;
Death followed with proud feet and smiling stare,
And the mad crowds ran madly up and down.

And many died and hid in unfound places
In the black ruins of the frenzied night;
And Death still followed in his surplice, white
And streaked in imitation of their faces.

*   *   *   *   *   *

But in the morning men began again
To mock Death following in bitter pain.

The Last of Pierrot

Pierrot again on octaves strums around,
(Octaves his only meaning, speech and measure),
White, wasted, wanton fool that kisses pleasure
Thinking with love's glass knife to stab the ground
And draw life-blood from out his painted heart;
Forgetting that its texture is but paper,
More fragile frills than gossamer or vapour,
A ribbon, tied with eighteenth-century art.

He sits and shivers on a tattered stool,
Hearing the cold grind out the endless breath
From saddened shadows: 'Sober now,' he saith,
'The cards lie upwards on the useless pool,
The drums are filled with blood and wine and lead,
Carnaval buried long, and Pierrot dead.'

Sonnet

This is no time for prayers or words or song;
With folded hands we sit and slowly stare,
The world's old wheels go round, and like a fair
The clowns and peepshows ever pass along.
Our brains are dumb with cold and worn with strife,
And every day has lingered on our faces,
Marking its usual course and weary paces
With cruel cunning care and sober knife.

Fate, like a sculptor working with great tools,
Now moulds his genius into clever ways;
Our souls are cut and torn all for his praise
When his great masterpiece is praised by fools;
But Death has beaten him, and takes the pride
From the strong hands that held us till we died.

War

And yet we live while others die for us;
Live in the glory of sweet summer, still
Knowing not death, but knowing that life will
Be merciless to them – and so to us.
Blood lies too rich on many battlefields,
Too many crowns are made for solemn sorrow;
We rise from weeping, and the cruel morrow
Has nought, but to a further sorrow yields.
No god is yet arisen, who with fair
Firm judgement shall arrest this course of war
And make destruction cease; say: 'Nature's law
Too long hath broken been.' None yet may dare
Hold out a mighty hand, bid Death withdraw,
Or break the current of this world-despair.

Monkery!

Oh multitude of popish monkery,
Give up your praying, spare your incense now,
For God has long forgotten your faint hearts
And your long self-inflicted suffering.
Give over challenging the wicked world

To steal your contrite souls from sacrifice;
This is no age of prophets, who with vows
Lived long in wildernesses, burnt at stake,
Or were translated into glorious heaven
Without the knowledgeable fear of death.
Put out the alter candles one by one,
Close down your sainted books and liturgies,
Untie the chaplets of your gathered beads,
And bow farewell to sanctity of church
(Recluseful ease wherein were spent your days).
This is a time of strife and war and death;
Against all these no prayers of man prevail;
But all the term of Time's impatience now
Is loosely rampant, and destruction comes
To burn and pillage what was long thought safe.
But when once more the passionate earth is bound
And quieted by plenitude of peace
There must arise a greater, truer life
Above the formula of mere religion;
And as the ancient order passeth ever
Into the transmutation of the new,
So must all practices of former days
Sink in the silent whirlpool of the past.

1917

The curtains of the sky are tightly drawn;
As in a horrid sunken maze the sun
Is veiled with wickedness, and all the streets
Shine horribly and wanly at noontide.
Now all the precious greenery of trees,
Remaining deaf to the command of spring,
Is still imprisoned by late lagging time;
And in the silence of the winter night

There are as yet no signs of moon or dawn;
And in the minds of men there is no hope,
No spark of courage to foresee the end
Of the long-reigning period of this war.

While like the murmur of a thousand clocks
Wild apprehensions crowd into the days,
And force their weary fingers at our throats.
There is no use in putting on a mask
And crying 'kamerad' to death and strife;
There is way to close our troubled hearts
To all the things that we have known before
(Yet then found loopholes to escape therefrom).
Each day a fever that's both new and old
Will come and struggle with our weariness.
And there will be no spring, no summer more
When the sweet smile of heaven rests on earth;
No faith, nor enterprise. Secretly still
We shall go slinking through the web of Time;
And when the war is ended, glorious dreams
That have been planned and nurtured with our blood
(Conceived of faith in blind futurity)
Will float unseizable from our weak hands;
And there will be no joy of road or sea,
No freedom of fresh countries and rich towns,
No glory in a peace that comes too late.

Promise

Had I a clearer brain, imagination,
A flowing pen, and better-ending rhymes,
A firmer heart devoid of hesitation,
Unbiased happiness these troubled times,
With pleasure in this discontented life,

Forgetfulness of sorrow and of pain:
Triumphant victory over fear and strife,
Daring to look behind, and look again
Ahead for all the slowly coming days:
See nothing but the carnivals of peace,
Forget the dreams of death and other ways
Men have imagined for their own decrease –
I'd write a song to conquer all our tears
Lasting forever through the folding years.

Lament

I am an angry child's last broken toy,
Left over from the games of yesterday,
Forgotten in a corner, cast away
By the tired hands of some small peevish boy.

I am a broken idol of last year,
Once worshipped richly in a golden shrine,
A deathless god that nations called divine,
Yet found another whom they did prefer.

I am an exiled king without his crown,
A dying poet with a tattered mask,
A starving beggar who may nothing ask,
And a religion that has been cast down.

Mood

Smoke-stacks, coal-stacks, hay-stacks, slack,
Colourless, scentless, pointless, dull,
Railways, highways, roadways black,
Grantham, Birmingham, Leeds, and Hull.

Steamers, passengers, convoys, trains,
Merchandise travelling over the sea,
Smutty streets and factory lanes –
What can these ever mean to me?

The Knave of Spades

You are the Knave of Spades; I swear you are
No other personage, no other card
In any pack has that satanic eye.
You are the soul of highway robbery,
And you have nimbly mocked at all those toys,
Pistols and crossbones, horses, masks and skulls;
For you have been too swift in every chase
And now you hover round forgotten gibbets,
Staring, and laugh. Again you are a wild
Great stamping Tartar full of ecstasy;
Your speech is suave, yet like a scimitar
Cleaves the white air with blazing irony.
I love you, Longhi's darkest lurking shadow,
Appearing suddenly, as quickly gone
Back to your eighteenth-century lagoons;
I am not sure *you* weren't that famous snake
That is accused of having tempted Eve
With apple-talk; (you knew how well to lie).
I hope that I shall never live to see
In your dark face the sign of any pain

Or any creeping sorrow that spoils pride;
(The pride of devils that may never suffer).
I think you have been king of your desires,
First granting them, then turning them to dust;
Weirwolf, enchanter, sometimes Harlequin,
A bitter Harlequin of curious moods
When midnight trembles and the West meets East...
God knows what more, but I prefer just now
To think of you as that same Knave of Spades,
A fiendish rebel with no heart; and yet
You are my love, the witchcraft of my faith.

Psalm

It makes you blind and mad; tears like a fire
Tears at the root of things, destroying all
Till the last flame is out, but love goes on.
Sometimes it gladdens you with valiancy,
Oh false fleet feeling that dies down too soon
Under the waters of reaction. True,
Love is a thing you shall not do without,
Nor having, hold it; bitter salted bread,
Disguised like shameful poison at a feast;
And those two brimming cups each side of you
Really contain the drunkenness of pain
And not the intoxicants of earthly wine.

You may not spurn this unknown hedge-row guest
That others jeer at, till he frightens them
With a thrown-off disguise; for love slips in
Behind you unawares. Some call him life,
The cowards call him death, and close their eyes
Under the ardent passion-flames of pain.

Love has the brave in his especial care,
And leads them open-eyed through all the worlds
Of hell and heaven; what wonder then if some
Go mad with climbing to such altitudes
Forgetting the descent? Heroes alone
Love takes for his unknown and ultimate ends,
And turns for them the thorns to passion-flowers
That never fade – immortalising love.

But dreary horny-handed fate sets out
Drawing the scattered back into the net;
And when the racing of the mill is done,
If love has pardoned you, and pitied you,
Comes from the wreck a phoenix, and you've got –
Friendship, that topmost solitary star.

Prayer

Oh God, make me incapable of prayer,
Too brave for supplication, too secure
To feel the taunt of danger! Let my heart
Be tightened mightily to withstand pain,
And make me suffer singly, without loss.
Now let me bear alone the ageing world
On firmer shoulders than the giant Atlas.
Make me symbolically iconoclast,
The ideal Antichrist, the Paradox.

Sirens

Your life – ship at sea, your moods – the winds,
The currents moving and the threatening rocks
That guard old fairylands of promises;
Those pleasant possibilities of Time
When the great seas go down and harbour seems
Of sure attainment, when the racing storm
And mangled foaming have been harvested
By the calm quietude of silent eves.
Then shall you see a port with welcome joy,
And trim the sails, steer on the craft with care.
The weary crew of your imaginings
Grown sceptical with suffering of salt waves
And striving days of stress and storm, now kneels,
And with a fervour got from prayers vouchsafed
Gives thanks to Fate. Oh false-illusioned souls,
The sanctity of harbour is too short!
You have forgot no ship has any home
Other than tumult; battling with the speed
Of the great multitudes and waves of thought,
The drastic hurricanes of huge emotion,
Despairing, long, flat calms of misery
when rowing fails – precipitous heights and deeps
Of wild mid-ocean madness, shifting sands
Where patience runs aground and perishes;
And yet you deem it freedom! Life at sea,
Tossed round forever, battered, staggering on
To finish voyages and recommence.
Better maybe at last unstop our ears
And follow the songs of sirens, guilelessly,
Down to the depths of some enchanted death
Where pain has been forgotten, tears shut out,
And old out-grown emotions turned away;
Where, like a miracle maybe, we'd find
Reflection of the same soft paradise,
Rare as on earth, but now attainable.

Evenings

Now when you hear the musing of a bell
Let loose in summer evenings, mark the poise
Of summer clouds, the mutability
Of pallid twilights from a tower's crest –
When you have loved the last long sentiment
Slipped onto earth from sunset, seen the stars
Come pale and faltering, the blaze of flowers
Grow dim and grey, and all the stuff of night
Rise up around you almost menacing –
When you have lost the guide of colour, seen
The daylight like a workman trudging home
Oblivious of your thoughts and leaving you
Silent beside the brim of seas grown still,
Placid and strange. When you have lingered there,
And shuddered at the magic of a moon
That will not sleep, but needs your vigilance
And seizes on the musings of your soul
Till you are made fanatical and wild,
Torn with old conflicts and the internal fire
Of passion and love, excessive grief of tears
And all the revolutions found in life –
What then? your body shall be crucified,
Your spirit tortured, and perhaps found good
Enough a tribute for some ultimate art.

The River Nene

Oh the eternal sweetness of the river
Under mysterious sunsets, creeping on
Through meadows flowerless and low; today
Sleeping they stretch in silent mellowness.
No April flowers are here, no butterflies

Trilling on spotted cowslips, for today
Nature's communion with the darkening season
Sets amber berries glowing, clustered birds
Whispering in autumn hedgerows. In the sky
Clouds meditate and slowly pass to westward;
The velvet greens are smoothed – I have walked long
Illumined by the purity of sunset
Soft as a kiss; stood on the gentle hills
And wondered at the world, this delicate
Sweet solitude of midland river valley
That wanders as a dream. I have gone by
The murmurous mill, the greyness of a village,
And loved the vesperal merging of the day
Into completed acquiescent night;
Found here the long reposeful altitudes
That guide the soul to heavens temporal.

Voyages North

The strange effects of afternoons!
Hours interminable, melting like honey-drops
In an assemblage of friends...
Or jagged, stretching hard unpleasant fingers
As we go by, hurrying through the crowds –
People agape at shops, Regent Street congested
With the intolerable army of winter road-workers
Picking; then in the Café Royal
Belated drunkards toying with a balloon
Bought from a pedlar – streets and stations
Serried together like cheap print, swinging trains
With conversational travellers arguing on the Opera –
Newspapers, agitation of the mind and fingers,
The first breath of country dispelling undue meditation
With the reposeful promise of village firesides;

Greetings at meeting – But if I were free
I would go on, see all the northern continents
Stretch out before me under winter sunsets;
Look into the psychology
Of Iceland, and plumb the imaginations
Of travellers outlandish, talking and drinking
With stern strange companies of merchants;
I should learn
More than one could remember, walk through the days
Enjoying the remoteness, and laughing in foreign places;
I should cure my heart of longing and impatience
And all the penalties of thought-out pleasure,
Those aftermaths of degradation
That come when silly feasts are done.
I should be wise and prodigal, spending these new delights
With the conviction of a millionaire
Made human by imagination – they should be
The important steps that lead to happiness
And independence of the mind; then should I say
Final farewell to streets of memories,
Forget the analytical introspection
And the subjective drowsiness of mind,
Stamping into the dust all staleness of things outgrown,
Stand on a northern hilltop shouting at the sun!

The Love Story

The time for fairy-tales is past; secure
The latch was shut on children's dreams, but one
Escaped, and daring fled into the world
Where growing magically, men called it Love…
In secret hurrying through the troubled nights
Like feverish criminals that fear pursuit
We hide the gold of our discovery,

Trembling to look on it; ah, where shall be
Time for the heart to rest and hands to hold
Untrembling all the treasure, breath be found
To conjure into life this stolen gain
And clasp it, willing fellow to our joy?
The shining bird that will not be constrained
Nor tamed with dazzling toys, the lightning flame
That strikes and shatters, the fiery paradox
That burns the soul into a sobbing sea
When all is done and the sweet story fled;
Then grow we old, and weary of all tales!...

Transmutation

This transmutation of the visible
Into subconscious feelings of the past,
And the insistence of declining autumn,
Mysterious vapour, latent colouring
Of humid clouds, clouds like a face aghast.
We breathe in memories, and the infinite loss
Of summer – Silences are like dumb grief,
Preying and long, woven with spell of tears
Come from untraveled regions, unexplored
By consciousness; this an instinctive day,
Dateless but poignant, solemnly subdued –
We are the prisoners of the sky and earth,
The suffering hostages of memory.

Love

Oh Love, shall we not leave you at the last!
We have exploited all your mysteries
And lures of glamour; time's corollary
Is heavy with our vows, our platitudes
Attempting happiness – love that was proud
And tightly clasped the honourable sword
Of disillusion to a passionate breast;
Adventurous love that would not be gainsaid,
And sought to storm the world with eloquence
Making a hero out of commonplace;
Or kindly love compassionate as sleep,
Pure as a song of peace, (a charity
That also has been spurned, unrecognised).
For we have suffered as the martyrs, sought
After your revelations secretly,
Trembling yet brave; we have put out of mind
The gaping mockeries of our defeat,
Thinking to climb a summit, dreaming then
To gather up some prize of recompense
In a new world untrammelled with horizon.
But all these roads are circular and dark,
Remote with loneliness, ending in nought
Beyond the cynical smile of memory...

*   *   *   *   *   *

Oh love, must we not leave you at the last!

Poor-Streets

They shall not know the tuneful words of love
Nor the impatience of imagination;
They shall not see the meaning of the day,
Nor slip into the comfortable dreams
Of which we make pleased profitable hours.
For they shall plod and shudder in the streets,
Shadowed by poverty's unending sadness;
Streets that are long and sullen, unrelieved
By smile of sunlight. Winter is your season
And all your meaning, suburbs! pale-faced skies
Shall weigh on you as lead – Oh, hideous poor,
Accursed of life, there is no explanation
Of fate incomprehensible! no clue
That I should sit by a secluded fire
And know the ending of your day will be
The desolate despair of public houses.

The Wreath

Love has destroyed my life, and all too long
Have I been my enemy with life, too late
Unlocked the secrets of existence! there
Found but ashes of a fallen city
Stamped underfoot, the temple of desires
Run through with fire and perished with defeat.
I would not speak the word of Disillusion
But have long felt the seal of melancholy
Stamped on my sombre autumn resignation.
My loves have been voracious, many-coloured,
Fantastic, sober, all-encompassing,
Have flown like summer swallows at the sun
And dipped into a wintry world of water:

Returned with laughing eyes or blenching face
From each horizon, from the Ever-New:
Passed through Adventure's net, struck at the stars
Flung by excitement recklessly so high:
Delved into precipices warily
And picked the jewel there from dragon-jaws:
Questioned the sphinx of Personality
Reading the puzzling riddles of the sand,
Bringing back prizes, bringing home defeat;
Sometimes to answers ancient questions turned,
Or driven on, flown like unbalanced moths
Round the perpetual candle of a sage,
Dropping to dust on Science's midnight.
They have gone forth like innocent crusaders
To win the ideals of mediaevalism;
They have set sail on roving western waters,
Searched for Eternity in worlds untame,
Fought for their lives against the rush of Time
And known the despairs of death, and war's dismay –
Of these my cunning crown is made, of these
Imperious leaves the sombre final wreath!

Sonnet

I have lost faith in symbols, wearily
Put out of mind their virtues stripped by Time;
Their magic sciences are gone from me,
Lost as a line that halts, a broken rhyme,
Dead as an ancient metre, dumb as thought
That may not be expressed: some tortured theme
That follows like a ghost, from memory brought
By the persistent power of a dream,
Unwanted, all recurrent – Where shall be,
When the last flame is out, ion found,

An explanation of philosophy
For they that live, or lie deep underground?
Oh, we shall never know, nor they be free –
Unanswered riddles move the world around...

Answer to a Reproof

Let my impatience guide you now, I feel
You have not known that glorious discontent
That leads me on: the wandering after dreams
And the long chasing in the labyrinth
Of fancy, and the reckless flight of moods –
You *shall* not prison, shall not grammarise
My swift imagination, nor tie down
My laughing words, my serious words, old thoughts
I may have led you on with, baffling you
Into a pompous state of great confusion.
You have not seen the changing active birds
Nor heard the mocking voices of my thoughts;
Pedant-philosopher, I challenge you
Sometimes with jests, more often with real things,
And you have failed me, you have suffered too
And struggled, wondering. The difference lies
In the old bulk of centuries, the way
You have been fashioned this or that; and I
Belong to neither, I the perfect stranger,
Outcast and outlaw from the rules of life,
True to one law alone, a personal logic
That will not blend with anything, nor bow
Down to the general rules; inflexible,
And knowing it from old experience;
So much for argument – *My* trouble is,
It seems, that I have loved a star and tried
To touch it in its progress: tear it down
And own it, claimed a 'master's privilege'

Over some matter that was element
And not an object that would fit the palm
Of a possessor, master-mind itself
And active-ardent of its liberty.

We work apart, alone; conflicting tides
Brim-filled with angers, violences, strife,
Each championing his own idealism,
Romanticism and sceptic bitterness...
The last I leave you, for this present mood
(The name of which you have expounded so)
Has turned against you, bared insulting teeth
And snarled away its rage into the smile
Of old remembrance: 'You were ever so,'
Exacting and difficult; in fact the star
That will not, cannot change for all the price
Of love or understanding – mark you *now*
I have concluded we are justified
Each in his scheming; is this not a world
Proportioned large enough for enemies
Of our calibre? Shall we always meet
In endless conflict? I have realised
That I shall burn in my own hell alone
And solitary escape from death;
That you will wander guideless too, and dream
(Sometimes) of what I *mean*, the things unsaid,
Vacant discussions that have troubled you
And left me desperate as a day of rain.

Then we shall meet at crossroads in wild hours
Agreeing over fundamental fates,
Calamities of a more general kind
Than our own geniuses have kindled up.
But at the fabulous Judgement day, the End,
We shall be separate still, and you will find
That Destiny has posted you once more
Back in the sky – and I shall be on earth.

Sonnet

What will you say of me if I should die
Without the last words spoken? Shall there be
Some brave religion that will testify
Belief in my strange faith, and bury me
As I would wish? with arms upstretched and high
Cold eyes turned seaward, souls symbolical
Caught in a prison still; they shall not die
But be mute audience to the logical
Denunciation of my life by you,
You, the calm critics, and the easeful wise
That have long done with doubt and take for true
That which is taught by faith, and seen with eyes,
Learnt from life's lessons – mourners will be few
That follow my last questioning surmise.

Western Islands

The islands of the blessed, the sunset isles,
Full of long summer, and the undying light
That pauses in its radiancy; and there,
The distant piping of some quavering music
That has expressed the lyric souls of gods
And the long loves of heroes – There have I seen
Isolda bearing Tristan on the waves
From rugged melancholy to dreaming death;
And syren-lovers weaving wreaths of song
Tuned to the tides, while poets slowly dream
The delicate tales of intermingling souls.
Now time breathes death and life, but leads all there
On the last western voyage of the sun,
All that is worthy of infinitude;
Heroes and lovers made immortal there

By the insistence of undying beauty.
In exultation shall we not approach
This mystic heaven that outstrips the stars?
And find anew the passions lived on earth,
Yea, without stress, but in beatitude.

The Haunted Castle

Outside, the staring eye of emptiness,
Eyes of the dead unclosed! What lovely sin
In long forgotten centuries within
Filled the glad rooms with transient happiness?
This castle is a husk of flowers dead,
This barren window has enclosed an hour
Saved from the world by love; alas, no power
Brings back for us these tales, romances sped
Down to the grieving sea, and out beyond
The last red clouds of sunset – empty rooms
Wait for new stories, wait with vacant eyes,
Eyes of the dead; the waves are ever fond
Of midnight sorrowing, and the castle looms,
Gaunt, without answer to the moon's surmise.

Thamar

Thamar in distant Georgia watched the sun
Set in voluptuous solitude; the hills
Brought to her lovers, and she bound their wills
Under her own firm spell, and every one
Of pleasure tasted, marvelled, and was dead:
Cast into night after a little hour
Of paradise incarnate, for her power
None might escape, by fate thereunto led.
But in the silent halls where love had lain,
Captive of all her beauty, wisdom, pride,
Rose clamouring ghosts that made her turn aside
Her longing eyes, as yet she waved again,
(Herself now prisoner of the loves that died),
Signal continuous o'er the endless plain.

Sublunary

1923

Sublunary

They are met at midnight in the windy tower,
Alchemist and students of alchemy,
Beneath a failing moon's reluctance; dark,
The narrow glen each side breathes mystery.
Moon without shadows streaming wan, and night
Again returning to its silences
After the laughing clamour of a fair,
The up-and-down of voices on the hill.
All these are past: they come to assignation,
In ruined chapel sit. Humbly at first,
The summer dews around them, solacing,
Each soul is lightened of its pain and made
Contemplative, desirous of hidden wisdom.
The master speaks, the crucible has grown
More red with throbbing secrets, dice are tossed
Till one has thrown the number winning speech.
He ponders daily thoughts, would know if friends
Are true when faithful words leap from their lips,
And if the heart should trustingly respond.
Then a newcomer, tantalising truth,
Voices the eager questionings of love:
'Shall every coin be spent, and every tear
Given from eyes revulsed in sacrifice –
And master, shall the profit outweigh loss?'
'But,' said another stranger, 'we know love –
How, treasuring it, our faith is kept serene;
Yet we are heavy with our uncertainties
Here on this brink of darkness – master, tell
Secret divine or clue we know not yet;
So that in dawns after most sorrowful dreams
We may unwrap ourselves from pain subconscious,
Making of haunted night a better day.'
'I have lost track of love,' another said.

Their ardent words assailed the midnight wizard,
And the dead saints looked down from their high walls,
At rest or dreaming still of the centuries past.
The moon grew yet more slight, ethereal, western,
And in the great world's streets thin cats and ghosts
Trod the transparent shadows, liberated
By this rare interval of dark and dawn.
So, full of striving each man told his tale
And would have known an answer to all things,
Thinking, 'we have that faith that walks the waves,
Faith of the holy parables indeed,
Tonight alone – a miracle shall reward.'
But they were given symbols, further doubts,
And stuff that fades with daylight; while the lord
Of their enchantment, wrapped in manifold mists,
Grown dim, was lost in far philosophies,
Unconscious to their calling. They were chilled
By the swift sudden wings of morning eagles
Stirring the empty space, and all the fire
Leapt in the crucible in one last flame
Of taunting laughter, fallen grey with ash.

Then from this company of questioners
That had adventured into wizardry
And sat around the stealthy science of truth,
Arose four friends and fled the haunted dew,
Descending silent to the dawn-white valley.

In a Café

Pale-face, turn round and look at me:
From out the shimmer of your glass
Are gone the indifferent that pass
Your fragile face. They cannot see,
Mark as I do, your weariness
Bowed to the music of this hour,
Unconscious, pensive as a flower.
Suppose I took for happiness
(All of a moment) your white face,
Lulled you with songs and gold – this place
Would surely fade from you and seem
But the persistence of sad dream?
Its music gone far from your mind
Ring as the voice of dull mankind,
Unheedful of your beauty – yet
When you awoke, the daily fret
And toil of living would return…
I am uncertain, while the tune
Urges me to you, and all soon
The hour is past us. Shall I spurn
The adventurous and fond certainty
That I might make of midnight hours,
With you, as soft as fairy flowers?
Pale-face turn round and look at me.

Eusebius Doubts

The pupil of the priests walks on the bridge
Pondering and ill at heart. Eusebius, young
Uncertain aspirant of the faith among
The docile clergy, gazes at that far ridge
High on the mountain where the sun is dying;
Thinks of the frolic springtime when the hours
Are sweet in meadows pale with cuckoo-flowers,
Dreams of young lovers laughing, birds low-flying
Over the mountain freshets. Then the bell
Rings him to vespers and to well-thumbed books;
His soul cries forth in anguish; Satan looks
Into his heart from out a neighbouring hell:
'Priesthood, Eusebius, thou shalt surely miss'…
Hurrying the tearful youth Christ's cross to kiss.

Iris of Memories

Do you remember in those summer days
When we were young how often we'd devise
Together the future? No surprise
Or turn of fate should part us, and our ways
Ran each by each; we picked the future's woof
Adventure searching, till these Sussex hours
Should bring us new adventure, while the flowers
About us waved in harvest plumes. Aloof
The house stood dark in green and gold of hay,
The house that we would leave fresh in the morn
To run the country on some quest forlorn,
Greeting the hop-pickers upon our way.
And there were wandering journeys to the sea
In dusty trains; there thrilling on the sands
Your scarlet dress grew vivid, and your hands

Evoked with witty gesture, palms of glee,
Things we had laughed at lovingly – for then,
Ah even then we loved our memories –
Till later under pale quiescent skies
We travelled homeward tired of towns and men,
Telling our dreams more slowly. So the moon
Crept up the stony hill between the hops,
(Full fields of ghosts become, where shadow stops
Across our stride); and all the stars of June
Breathed up the poignance of unbounded roses.
We heard the rustle in the sombre trees
Heavy with bats and owlish noise; the breeze
Brought on its flutter sound of gate that closes
Far in a meadow. Sometimes you would tell
Stories to chill one in this midnight hour,
Until your fancy trembled at the power
The story held to frighten you as well.
The air grew full of dawn and we would yet
Talk of our morrows and our yesterdays;
Outside the birds grew tremulous with praise
In the hot sunrise. We shall not forget
The slumbering hours of hayfields where the river
Between its hedges near the passing train,
Faltered unseen and voiceless, then again
Flowed out with dipping birds and fish aquiver;
For here we wandered silent, read strange things,
And had, how often, many a verse essayed,
Truant unfinished poems – as they played
Their shadowy game in the mind's fairy-rings,
Unseizably they mocked at our endeavour.
Then were there later days, with autumn rain
Damp in the haunted house, and so again
You would become a legendary inventor;
Weaving dark plays by firelight till sunset,
And thunder passing hence great moths came out
Sealing the redescended calm no doubt…
Iris of memories we shall not forget.

Mary Queen of Scots

From the Queen's Quiar

The little throat in ruffle of stiff gold,
The impatient tear that creeps through her suspense
In chapel ecstasy, the while her cold
White face in anguish turns to the immense
Remoteness of the northern solitudes,
Tasting the exile; then the teeming days
Of court adventure while her sorrow broods,
Heavy with tragedies. Her spirit prays,
Made ardent, and in hot uncertainty
Accepts sweet page's love and ruffian lover –
So is her longing warm at sudden fire,
Hid from the jealous storms that go above her
Drawing more close about her destiny,
Until the ending to such heart's desire.

Ballad of 5 Rue De L'Etoile

When you are dazed with antics of the street,
And weary of its tumult, and the fleet
Of turbulent traffic, faces, gestures, cries,
Turn to a dipping alley where the skies
Remoter seem from the intemperate light,
And here spend cooler hours until the night;
Pausing within a street of downward coil
That slinks obscurely from the vast Etoile.
All at your hand that you may wish for: take
The succulent fruit-store opposite to slake
Parched eyes with scarlet colour and fresh green.
When to my room you've climbed, and having been
Struck for a moment by fantastic deer

That on my curtains dance, turn patient ear
To story of the house and those that dwell
Discreet behind their pearl-grey walls and sell
Some, their light loves, and some, their willing brain.
For we are motely as a summer train
Is motley with its eager passengers
Ardent for seasides and the country stars.

I'll tell you how the women come and go,
Seemly and neat – for love will have it so;
Love that must climb some narrow midnight stair
Up several floors, demands good comfort there,
And comfort finding maybe will return –
And so their eyes can laugh, their lips can burn
With many a passion patiently (though then
Their thoughts may longing turn to other men);
Yet life has put them here and brought success,
Out of their minds are gone the days of stress,
And beauty is well served, and love as well.

Behind this silent door is one who'll tell
one day his vivid stories to the world,
Woven in poetry; yet now is furled
In brooding subtleties and runs the town,
Well-pleased returning arm-in-arm with dawn.
Then in hot sleepless nights no doubt revolves
Past dubious pleasures and makes new resolves;
Forgoing cafés and on work intent,
Those times forgetting, ill or swiftly spent
By oily river of mid-afternoons
Or light half-sinister of Paris moons,
Such things, and joys insidious of the heart…
Yet with all these it being hard to part,
Goes out when weariness has been refreshed
To lovely Paris that has his soul enmeshed
Now for some season.

Then on higher floors
Live unknown behind their closed grey doors
That bar curiosity – all these I deem
Go light-foot, heavy-heart; as in a dream
Pass companies with half-remembered faces,
Silent, unmeddlesome to other places,
Nothing to you or me in this retreat,
Less than the cobbled noises of the street –
They are the background to our liberty,
So that with fresher steps our destiny
This Paris June, through all the streets a-flower
Advance toward us in the evening hour.

Memory at the Fair

I knew not whence my sorrow came that night,
For we were dumb together sorrow and I,
Walking the Paris streets, until a cry
Rose from an autumn fair. I saw the white
Smoke curled above the noise of those bright places
Where spin the fortune-wheels; in flying swings
I rode the frosty air, and tossed the rings
At gaudy prizes. But in the darker spaces
Beyond this fiery turmoil stood my dreams:
Once ancient memory like a ghostly clown
Peered grimly at the scene with many a frown,
Grimacing disenchantment – for it seems
He mourned the past, adventurous time of chance,
Whispering to me, 'Where is now Romance?'

Adolescence

I am in years almost the century's child,
At grips with still the same uncertainty
That was attendant to me at the school.
The classics set before us, twenty voices
Took up enunciation, I was dumb –
Then goaded by the teacher's stony finger
Trembling arose to read a meagre essay.
Next History went by, its wars and glories,
And politics that fill young minds with dust
Or Corn-laws and Reform – severe decades
When England topped the century with Victoria.
But we might never know Queen Katharine
Who ruled imperially adventurous in Russia,
Nor hear the Borgias' crimes, the papal swindles;
For us no pages on the Medicis,
No panorama of past things in Rome,
But thorny sums, and German verbs rapped out.
For Art we had the photographic torsos
Of Jove and all his Venuses, with words
That lay less easy on the lecturer's tongue:
We never doubted that her themes were Whitman,
Browning and Wordsworth – here we had examples,
Morals and principles… ('Now these two terms
Must be explained to show you've understood.')
The winter spent at this came Tennyson.
By half-past twelve all done the rest would go
With confident memories, but I forgetful
Scattered the lesson's fragments in the street,
And hated life, with adolescent sense
Of wrong that dallies with tearful introspection.
I knew I could not learn, despite the prize
Between my hands the day that I was free.

*   *   *   *   *   *

That summer went in solitude, with thoughts
Humming in concourse, as the thronging stars
Appear before the eyes of travellers
Descending to new lands on hurrying feet.
If at some time each man says: 'world is mine,'
Then doubtless rang this clamour in my heart,
And many a fire was lit and worshipped there,
Ascetically, with pride, and so with longing.
I held the very world's perplexities,
Throbbing of questions, stirring of heart's blood
Urging hysterical things till dawn had come.

     *   *   *   *   *   *

A year of riot grew, with carnivals,
Music and wines beneath the million lamps
That flanked the thresholds of advancing war.
There were no ruins yet; each hour was gold
That reddened in the fires of its adventure –
Then had I thought of aftermaths, and stood
Uncertainly between the opened gates
Scanning the crossroads of a violent world.

The April Hour

The eagle above a cloudless solitude,
The wan grey rocks and songless silent spaces –
Here wandered lovers happy, old at heart,
Young with life's pulsing in their sorrow-freed eyes,
Moved through late-shadowed glades and spokes of spring.
The early year had paused, and turned to radiance
This delicate hour of love; so were we calm,
Borne on the glad fulfilment of the moment,
Half-kin with the high soaring of the eagle.

Premature Spring

Let us go out my love to the strange spring weather,
See how the jonquils stiffen upon the lawn;
I have picked the first – from its triple garland of yellow
A fragrance is wafted to us on the uppermost terrace,
Hand-clasped and exultant, at gaze on the mists of the sea.
Though a nebulous morning has risen, its clouds and its shadows
Will part in the delicate sunshine – ah, see how they flow
Far back to the mountains, revealing a tender horizon
Uncertain as yet in the tremulous flush of the tide…
And here in the grass adolescent that thrills with the spring
Let us dream for a while of this hour, we are one with these things.

Sonnet

Here at the cross-roads we will part as friends
Going a little journey from each other;
Shoulder your memories, and I will gather
In these fresh fields all things that fortune sends
For when I find you next. Thus in some street
We know not yet, or in some autumn valley
Being met again, our thoughts as one will sally,
That all our partings make reunion sweet.
Far sweeter than the unbroken melody
That we must play each hour, each night, each dawn,
Till all our notes be spent and singing gone –
What use in songs enforced, what harmony?
But good are the adventures found alone
That we shall tell, no longer solitary.

Mist

When in the formal silence settled suddenly
Flutter strange thoughts within a room of mirrors,
Which shall we cling to, which shall we forget?
Memories of hours gone hither, words of daylight,
Now in the glimmering night, the night of mirrors,
Unpitied martyrs of their forced reflections.
Spray on sea, wan winter leaves blown skyward
Traceless remaining – Even as the dust
Rises oblivion merciful, and the gleam
Fades from the mirrors with our departing faces.

In the Valley of Willows

There is a mystery in the willow tree,
It sways in tremulous tide of light and shadows
Over the many waters where I see
This summer float upon a stream of shallows,
Curling about the pools whence lilies come.
By these in brooding twilight hour I dream
Of willow's secret, and walking see them dumb,
So faint in valley-mist that now they seem
Wreathed spirits risen for sorrow or for warning.
Nature's mythology is in their leaves
That flush with gold upon the crest of morning,
More vivid than laurel crowns that history weaves
In every century for her heroes dead.
It is of other stories they would tell,
Bending and pensive, each with tufted head
Borne as a sheaf of waves on noon's hot swell
When breezes sing to them, and stir the great
Hillsides with harmony.

The forest trees
Are dark behind an imperial harvest's state.
A dim horizon circles; there, to please
The fervent eyes of travellers, go by
Pale happy clouds that hesitate and drift
Caressing earth, until the evening sky
Floats in with growing shadows, then they lift
White bosoms to the sunset and are gone,
Processing in swan-state to other spheres.
In mutability of autumn tone
An ambered willow bends, the valley fears
Great winds blown overland or from the sea.

I will not listen to the leaf that stirred
Uneasily, first herald of what must be
When all the winter's shouting gales are heard.

At Martin-Eglise

Beyond these buttercups of summer fields,
Past willows grey with light and poplars trembling,
I see the heavy woods' green waves dissembling
Dark fancies and dark shadows; then it yields
A sudden road that curls about the valley,
Threading the golden grasses and the corn.
Here is a chorus to arouse the morn,
Bird-voices thrilling – here the fish that dally
Between the currents of a wayward stream.
In these long August hours I fall to musing,
Weaving of stories that will never be,
Till sombre grows the wood. Then shall I dream
Once more those memories that brook no choosing,
Wave upon wave arising as at sea?

Bottles, Mirrors and Alchemy

A room of oak, ascetic; panelled walls
With here and there a faded ancestor
Of whom they tell dark legends – hints at cross-road
Robbery, and fables of midnight daring;
Dark in the shadow hang the portraits grim.
Behold a mirror that has seen last century
Pass laughing in to many a Christmas banquet,
Clouded before the eyes of weeping damsels
That were sequestered here, or crossed in love –
And now it shines for us: I hazard questions.
'How is it you have kept those flagons still,
Bottles and demi-johns the firelight plays on?'
'Some eighteenth-century Falstaff held them last,
We drink in smaller measure...' Your voice is silent.
And so I look between the four tall candles
And sink into a latent zone of fancies;
Knowing the winter winds outside the pane,
The mirrors hiding memories, mocking us.
It seems in their perspective I can see
An old-time alchemist at work on things:
Disordered golds and dross lie at his feet,
And doubt has stemmed his feverish research.
Look, here's a vial full of scalding purple,
Broken in anger, bubbling with scattered atoms –
'Have you the toad's eye, Wizard – viper's tongue,
And secret incantations for the foe
That you are moulding as a waxen puppet?'
Oh – while this owl is hooting you are gone...
That haughty purple is a bottle staring
Now dim, now flaming, on the distant dresser;
Bottles we have not touched... The room grows darker;
And from the corners creep delicious mice,
Pink-pawed and shadow-grey; then the avenger,
Puss from her slumber woken, scenting game.
I cannot keep my ears and thoughts intent,

Friend, on your drowsy pointless information;
And sink into the great beatitude
Your room has put upon me – till the word
'Haunted…' and here's a trinity of candles!
The fourth has died. Oh I will close the book
Of my imagination, let the leaves
Fly back in helter-skelter to their covers,
Though all the mirrors still are brimming visions
For him that hath eyes to see – You did not say
Till then the room was haunted… Now am I
Prisoner of yours, well pleased and half afraid.

Drought

This day is long at dying, and tarries yet
Late in the harvest fields, until the sun
Brooding a fierce decline is gone at last,
Flinging broad arms across the western waters.
Softly the twilight breathes upon the earth,
Distils grey glimmer on the giant corn
And on the heavy sheaves, where flaming hours
Have gilt and browned and burned the dying pastures.
July, the soul of summer, the month imperial,
Dispenser opulent of all good things,
Is turned incendiary, stays not his fire;
And every night must languish until dawn,
Watching the moon bear hence that mocking gold,
That lovely spurious gold of her cool face
That lies aloof in distant contemplation.

Shall We Forget?

When we must go our ways no more together
After this shortening time that love has given
Our hearts to meet, remember that day of driven
And wayward rains, soft lulls in the wild weather,
And we on the road, full-hearted with mute lips
Masking the sorrow each should have of each
Once all things told. We saw the meadows reach
Wet arms about the river where it slips
To quietude, and dies within the lake.
These waters, where two swans wove silently
Their twin romance of summer's harmony,
Heard your confession's ardour, saw us make
The delicate vow of love, though you are bound
Now on another quest, and faithfully
Go to its call; so in desire we found
Immortal hope wrought with uncertainty.

In the Valley of Arques

Wave upon wave the forest moves, descending,
Stemmed in the valley by the sun-flushed corn;
Here in hay-harvest lie the meadows bending
Ripe tapestry of grasses that are shorn
Soon, all too soon; thus goes the vast long day
Seeing granaries grow and grass piled up in stooks
Beside the road to Arques where poplars sway
Drowsing above the prairie's welling brooks.
The summer winds are with us, and their motion
Urges pale clouds to sunset, there for gilding,
And distant sounds come inland from the ocean,
Fade in the evening mists that earth is yielding
Wave on ethereal wave, and very white
The valley waits for each enfolding night.

The Siege

All day the crowds have battered at the gate
That frowns, unyielding to their anger still;
One solitary sentinel is left
At guard upon the walls, armed with resistance.
The tranquil morning of a weary spring
Woke to the sudden clamour of enemies
That surged rebellious, with implacable cries
From each calm corner of the far horizon,
Baying like ravenous hounds that thirst for slaughter.
At noon they wrestled with lurid mouths agape,
And sprang again in that glow of agony
The sun lets fall before his royal death.
Now in the evening has the sentinel,
Lonely survivor above the battle-ground,
Faltered, dismayed with languor in the struggle.
The hiding king, whose courtiers fled, now sees
Himself the weary prisoner of his castle,
Moves out upon the battlements, speaks sheer
To his last partisan; still the ordeal
Rages beneath them – and round my heart as well.
The castle is my heart, and I the prisoner
That moves towards the sentinel of his hope.
The lances of memory and apprehension
Are sharp about us in the darkening twilight;
But we have built our walls of stuff immortal,
Their roots go deep in soil of eternity –
Yield not, for life grows strong from such endurement!
So do we cry to each other, and face anew
The sweeping battalions of adversity.

Twelve Chimes upon the Clock

Twelve chimes upon the clock; in such an hour
Did Faustus clamour for his bartered soul
Till midnight rang, and God had heard him not.
At such a time was Macbeth murderer,
And heard the heavy wind proclaim his deed
In sombre rooms – The Dutchman out at sea
Departs again, fleeing with his despair
From the last love that might have won him peace.
Now from the shadow torn by vengeful moon
Falters Don Juan before the stern Commander,
Marching to hell, condemned for boasts of old –
The visionary ponders through the night
And sees their histories go by once more
Haunting, though sealed with death's atonement now.

Horns in the Valley

This June the nights lay heavy until dawn;
Then did my heart devise in solitude
Of old romances – came an evocation
Across the valley mists at sound of horns
Deep in the forest springing. So again
When the last chord had died, Isolda rose
With pulsing signal of imperious arms
Uplifted in long tremolo of passion.
I saw the grasses bend before her lover,
Precipitate wraith that hurried to her calling;
And the lost echoes of their ardent voices
Grew in my sense with fading of the horns,
Sighing an ultimate song of death and love.
Then in the harbour of the risen moon
The dew lay solitary; no shadows there

Guarded these pale-faced lovers through the night,
And the lone tower was empty of its watcher.
But in that moment were they joined at trysting,
Come to the cadence of this midnight music,
And now are gone on silence desolate.

Here is the Autumn

Here is the autumn moving with gaunt strides
And moody gestures, rain is in the skies.
Within the little house are sighing dreams
That last no longer than a restless minute,
Yet ever again arise like those frail leaves
That are so still before the winds awake;
The tempest hurries them from the far forest
And from my apple-trees – leaves of regret.
There is no pattern to this autumn hour
Brooding in luminous grey uncertainty
Beneath a cloudy sky prepared for battle.
All things cry out to me, 'Make ready now
Without farewell to leave the coming storms,
Hasten before the trembling apples fall;
The leaves are turning, and these days must end
When the last fruit is parted from the tree.'
Yet I would rather listen to the winds
That will encompass this decline, indeed
The ultimate farewell is very close.

If We Devise Tonight –

The misty night is breathing, it is time
Now before dawn to light forgotten candles
That wait to hear our last philosophies.
There is a singing in my heart, a crying
To all the muted restlessness of autumn –
If with replenished glasses we should speak,
Discourse upon such things, tell other thoughts,
Uncoiling the wound treasure of our fancies?
The moth with folded wings inside this room
And the wild bats of darkness, no other hosts
Will come to our devising; I hear you say:
The depths that we would touch are still unplumbed
As we descend the passage of our moods
Sowing our thoughts upon the silence – No,
We shall not gather truth save in our dreams
That waking end upon the word 'perhaps.'

Adventurer

When we go hence will all our memories
Linger or hasten in the hurrying hour,
Shall they take up the burden of our moods,
Carry dead days towards us as we go,
Fled from the flying hours that were our friends?
Storms lie around us – shall we ever touch
The stationary beacon of far flames
Poised in the distance of an unknown sea?
Adventurer born so shall adventurer end
In hot uncertainty of each new hazard.

The New Friend

'Good-Night' you said to me, and down the street
Went the uncertain cadence of your footsteps
Slowly at first, then was the night between us,
So did I turn, and followed in my mind
All the perplexities that would attend you
For company upon the little stair
You have not known as yet, for you had said
'I will not keep my weariness at home,
Rather pace through the night, and contemplate
In some new room the face of my despair –'
I saw your hours go by in loneliness
With saddening chimes of clocks; the crooked roofs
Would lie before you at the opened window,
Calm in thee dawn that should engender peace
Could you but curb your spirit's revolution.
There had been songs before our midnight's parting,
Adventures told, and future plans to be –
A southern journey far from all of these
People that drink with one till closing-time,
Voicing their numerous melancholies – then
The picture mocked us from the café walls,
Seemed as the laughter of departed companies.
I met you yesterday… Tonight as yet
Is blue before the lamps of seven o'clock;
I wait in the crowd that gathers, see crisp leaves
Slowly descend upon the Boulevard,
And think of country woods where dew is cold.
Here in this long September of the town
The lights are lit before our eyes shall meet
Again, before our voices ring together
Until they cease on echoing farewells.
We are two strangers come from distant places,
Driven on different tides whose turning currents
Have now assembled us – what purpose hides
In meetings that so soon must be put by,

Stored up with other memories in the mind?
I argue thus, while neighbouring tables fill
With those unconscious of the hour's suspense
That has drawn out my thoughts till you come by.

Sonnet

Not till the fruit is gold upon the tree,
Not till the flowers die and leaves are falling
Lightly within the fields, and swallows calling
Their summer broods about them to the sea;
Calling their April lovers to make ready
For the perpetual journey of each year;
Not till the days grow dark – ah do not fear
That I should leave you. As each hour the steady
Warm flush of summer makes the earth immense
In utter loveliness within our sense
So shall the treasure ripen of my love.
But for the waning days, ah sweet, prepare
A passionless farewell, no cry or tear
In those far times shall my departing move.

The Spiders Weave

The summer days were harsh with drought;
On earth there was no movement left
Beyond the apple's fall, when out
Of those dry husks the spiders crept

Listless with weaving. In my mind
It seemed that other spiders ranged,
Subconscious thoughts that struggle blind,
Laced with desires – they interchanged

For dreams the restraint our solitude
Enforces in the waking hours.
A vision grew, of one that stood
Alone upon the sunset's towers,

Warning with prophecies. He told
Of weary heart all dry with waiting;
How in an hour when life is cold
Life's enemy is contemplating

A cunning ruse and casts his snare,
And how of this dark vagabond
The heart must ever be aware,
Stern to the danger. Far beyond

The vision of that mystic wall
Rang out imperious accents: take
All that tomorrow's fate lets fall,
So that maybe some wind will shake

Things better far than apples green
Down to your waiting hands – I dreamt;
The spiders wove again their keen
Dry webs, and stalked the earth unkempt.

§

PROVENCE

Southward

Three passengers around a weary fly...
The vapid fly attacks the travellers
Buzzing the story of its own loneliness.
Drowsing we travel, see the autumn velvets
Lone of all stars outside – the hardy light,
Our luggage strapped, sophisticated, neat;
Pictures of Switzerland, Rivieras luring
To those who contemplate that holiday;
The lace above the seats, the dreary lace
That mocks God knows how many a man's insomnias,
Stemming his memories with interruptions.
Thoughts fret and gnaw me – through the corridors
Are blown the little empty winds of night
Bearing unrest and hunger – after these
At length tomorrow some dark line of trees
Sprung from the dawn. Propitiating South,
Provence shall meet us on her white highroads
Hot with the suns of yesterdays – ah cypress,
Already rising in the memory,
Cypress of plains I greet you with my longing,
Now in this hour so very still outside
The train must seem as flitting of the moth
Hung for a moment at the station's light;
And in the carriage one is patient, numb,
And two are still imprisoned in their sleep
Dreaming impossibly a thousand things...
Alone the fly is conscious of its life.

Beaucaire

High in this garden set against the south
The autumn trees are still about the towers,
Bowed by some vanished wind of winter hours
We have not known, and at the river's mouth
An estuary awaits the quiet sea.
There is a chime of bells like waters falling,
The circling pigeons flowing to their calling
Wheel through the sun. A pale monotony
Of clouds departing from the day is here;
And from the southern mists the very clear
White faces of the ruins rise again –
But I am destitute of phantasies
Wherewith to people their lost destinies,
Sufficient now this hour above the plain.

At Les Baux

It is the hour of meditation – listen,
As thought grows still the very bells are still
Upon the folded flocks; beneath this hill
Silent the road turns grey with night. Ah hasten
You little winds of evening and be gone;
Restless are you with fears, ghosts of suspense
Before the moon surrounds you with immense
Pale shrouds of light. This crescent moon alone
Moves in the fading ocean of the sky,
Save where in sorrowful west the colours die
As if eternally – their sheaves are pressed
In flames together, and the perpetual rocks
Pale ruins now, asleep as other flocks
Deep in the silence of the centuries rest.

To Vaucluse Came Petrarch and Laura

Follow this valley to the mountain's edge
Hung in immensity above the stream;
There in your climbing see the imperious ledge
With brooding castle crowned, where only a gleam
Of springtime fills the vacant ruins now,
And every summer seals the fountain's rush:
There was a time of pilgrims come to bow
And dip their faith in the miraculous gush.
Such fervent days as these Petrarch withdrew
With Laura dreaming, both fled from zealous life;
Each year upon this rock they met anew
In secret joy, remote from wordly strife.
Great lovers were they, so I like to think,
At rest upon their mountain's perilous brink.

At St Rémy

By St. Rémy, at parting of the ways,
Two jewels lie, old sculpting of Roman hands,
As thoughts on the background of a giant brain.
Time lingers here; each drop of southern rain
Effaces listless, tardily disbands
The pressing cohorts of forgotten days,
They move to battle still. And in a high
Clear cupola two figures crown the sky,
Placid in noble peace – a conqueror's mood
Ordained them, eternal witness of great hours;
The summers gild them, and the breath of flowers
Rises about their ardent solitude.
Today the winds assailed them as I stood
In desert groves and winter's empty bowers.

Saintes Maries-De-La-Mer

They heard God's radiant voice upon the deserts
Bidding them rise and northern countries seek;
Mary and Mary-Salomé the meek
Set sail with fervent heart to gain new converts,
Traversed those ardent tempests firm with faith,
Landing in wail of wind and furious waves
Where the great Rhone breaks free: their holy graves
Are consecrate and hallowed in ancient death.
The gales of these savage lands now smooth their dreams
In the stern tombs built for them, and at last
Their saintly sorrows are fled into the past;
A crowd kneels at their sanctuary and deems
Repose perpetual cradles these two fair
Adventurous Saintes Maries-de-la-Mer.

By the Dordogne

Leaving Cahors I go through feathery fields
Of ancient mustards golden to the sun,
They sway as if in mockery, where one
Grey steeple rises angrily and shields
A humble village with its shade severe.
Today the Dordogne valley, green and flush
With myriad flowers, slumbers in the hush
Of noon; spring's coffers have been emptied here.
I pause at sunset on the giant plains,
Where sheaf of pigeons on the wind up-blown
Wheels with fierce feathers through the hurrying skies
That stream above the earth; the evening rains
Hot light on these far furrows that are sown
With growing harvests, green before the eyes.

The Night in Avignon

The city's politics grow very loud
In this café, and the Provençal crowd
Drifts in, drifts out, while gestures intertwine
Throbbing against the giant mirrors; wine
Goes by on platter, hurrying waiters stand,
Arrested by the intoxicated hand
Of a southern orator, who drops his talk
To stare at the intruding stranger's walk.
Here are the women too, the local belles,
An aged adventuress that proudly swells
In dark immaculate satin, fashion's latest,
Flanked by a dozen men, for she's the greatest
Dame of the streets – the waiter whispers fast,
Relentless, till I go, thinking, at last
From crowds anonymous one must depart;
Walking away a little tired at heart,
Disturbed and baffled by the arguments
That ring as clocks and chime their discontents,
Sighing the hour that's lost, the hour that's gone
Into the silence of the dark. Oh town,
Home of tonight, Provence of autumn be
More than a threshold transitory to me,
With tenor voices ringing through the street
Above the accompaniment of many feet,
The urgent steps, the saunterings of the crowd
That stir vexation now. I'd cry aloud
Against the very suavest company
That would not leave me wilful, solitary,
This hour or two – for I could never write
With one beside me waiting, while the night
Unrolls its silent velvets in the street.
This is the time when hardy travellers meet
To gorge in taverns lustily, with wine
Of Chateau-Neuf des Papes, and sit in a line
Telling each other ready tales outside.

The plane-trees turn more ashen, very wide
The spaces in between the stars are grown,
With slip of moon imprisoned there till dawn;
But here, in the worldy cell, a game of chess
Holds two opponents pompously, a dress
Of orange stirs the mirrors with its flames
Startling my silence, while a voice proclaims
A stormy knowledge of the fate of France.
Tomorrow I'll be gone – the hours advance
To winter while the autumn's voices sing
Of drifting leaves, of many a beating wing
That hastens, travelling to the south each day.
The cypress avenues and the poplars sway
Clouded with risen dusts of winds returning.
I see white Avignon tomorrow burning
As beacon blond upon the sunset; last
The papal towers fade into the past
That steals them from me – but in another year
I shall turn back, and see, and hold, and hear
That which I have tonight, best things of France
That ripen in the harvests of Provence.

New Coasts

The memories of this coast are thick about me
Returned from springtimes past, and now the sunset
Fades, I pause in silence, looking back
At other days. I knew that garden first,
In its grove of ponderous trees where shadows lay
Deep on the afternoon, walled in with flowers
That trailed their burden of colours over-ripe;
Thus first the south ascended in my heart.
There was another time, in land of rocks
Flung broadcast to the sea, with Africa,

Giant unknown across the azure storms;
Great trumpetings were there in every crest
Crowning the ebb and plunge of wave and wave.
A bitter pine tree stood, cold as in prayer,
The hermit sorrowing in this wilderness
For arid soul cast out. Here was no green,
No living lovely thing beneath sky's blue,
Only a ledge for devil and for God
To meet again, a place of miracles;
So did this land seem holy ground. That day,
Between the mountains of the mists and dews
I took the road that climbs to Castillon,
High on its ruins poised – the old, the new,
Both gazing down upon the valleys. There
All things alive were in diaphanous trance;
The sun above the hill, and the white wraiths
Low on the lemon fields – no echo passed
Till distantly a flock of watery bells
Uprose and faded, leaving the altitudes
Remoter still in a religious twilight.

Now I have come to other coasts, and see
The luminous Alps at bay before the tide,
Their mystic line drawn out; the ocean swells,
Wary with treacherous blues, white crests unfurled,
And hurrying waves that race behind each other.
I note the unfriendly pines, trim egoists
That grow as spare as a long line of facts;
The olive trees that bow with curling arms,
Ripe with the glamour of the legends still,
They too are here – and vigilant on the terrace
One palm tree, deputy from Africa.

Red Earth, Pale Olive, Fragmentary Vine

Red earth, pale olive, fragmentary vine
Mellow with sun's decline.
In aftermath of harvest all the days
Are flushed with stillness, lit with almond greys,
And this November afternoon I see
Cypress against the sky so very still.
Upon a narrow strand
Full surges moving to the barren land
Towered with rocks, and on this sudden hill
I pause before the sunset that shall be,
In its last hour, a psalm
Sped to the journeying heart that seeketh balm.

The Solitary

And so I sit and let the hours pass
Huddled before the page and scarce awake;
In this deserted place there is no glass
To ring with mine, only still nights to slake
My thirsty craving with their lassitude.
And in the silence two caged birds are sleeping,
The fire is out, the hidden spiders creeping
Into the house along the rotted wood.
The very long complete decay of this,
Spreading its tangled cobwebs to the noon!
A dusty cypress broods, this shanty is
Only a ravaged husk beneath the moon.
There is no sound inside, and by the dead
Embers of hearth my wingless thoughts are still,
Cradled in ashes; nothing stirs until
I hear life's maggot gnawing its last shred.

Pale Moon, Slip of Malachite

Pale moon, slip of malachite
Above the smoke of the clouds poising
In a green moment that will not last –
And you there, far beyond the furthest roads and sea paths,
Distiller of the heavens,
One drop of blood in the sky, suffusing it:
Sunset, advancing
From this grey weather suddenly.

Tempests

In the alleys of the sea are companies of voices
Wailing ghosts' orisons, stirred within their tomb;
Storm on crest of ocean, tempest in the darkness:
Mortal hearts are quaking,
Destinies are hurried
Deathwards to the silence of immemorial gloom.

Storm within the heart when memories are driven
From their opened prison as gales before the past;
Equinox of passions lifting all before it:
Many a bonfire flaming
Lit by this rebellion,
And every door broke open that had been shuttered fast.

The Paradise's angels, the spirits buried deep
Far out in desert places are risen in alarm;
Apocalypse with trumpets clarioning Infinity:
The heavens at their quaking,
The stars in a last riot,
And we, a little fragment upon God's weary palm.

Echoes

The wandering footstep on the stair,
The waiting hour that leads to sleep,
A smile, then there is time to weep,
And after tears time to despair.

A summer moon forgotten now,
The brief adventure of two lovers,
An autumn stretch of cloud that covers
The windy starveling trees that bow

Sighing in sorrowful September –
And then the stillness of the street
That bears away the stranger's feet...
These things are lonely to remember.

Toulonnaise

She was a rebel governess
Who came from Toulon in the south,
Red cherries tumbling on her hat,
Loud laughter breaking at her mouth.

Came to the Midlands there to teach
A girl of seven sullen-hearted –
Her voice was full of life's adventure,
Her eye too gay, so she departed.

And I, the child of seven, wonder
In what far province of the south
After these years may rediscover
The cherries defiant of her mouth.

Lips that would snap with scorn then soften,
Chasing the scolding from her brow...
Thus I remember – comes the thought
We should not know each other now.

A Vis-à-vis

I shall never forget the ancient courtesan
Of Bandol by the sea, a little town
Lost in that Mediterranean saison morte,
With its hostelry that treats small fry en pension.
Her florid face blinks at an early dinner,
Poor solitary meal she knows so well
Without pretence of book or conversation,
Drawing her scarf about her. Very still,
The venerable false cat, she sums one up,
And does not savour the varied memories
Of those that filled her life; the moonstones gleam
In a golden setting upon each heavy arm,
Spoils of the past – If she would only tell,
Speak out the meagre mockeries of her mind!
Disapprobation peers from her eyes, and there
Is an acid smile as well, if smile be needed
Even now to dismiss inopportunities.
I think we angered her, as from the room
Between our voices shrilled, mosquito-like,
She moved in panoply of ancient taffetas.
But we forgot, flushing with local wines
Aided with metaphysical words, perhaps,
Forgot for an hour this siren of last century –
And then I saw her, sitting a little while
Before that tideless sea, alone, alone,
Spider at brood, now lulled in an intense
Malicious contemplation of the moon.

Spenkler

Spenkler in an overcoat
Perambulates galoshed thoughts
On little bridges, while we float
Beneath inquiringly. He sorts

The best in Venice from second-best;
'People are hard to mix,' he fears –
Dispensing tea at home he'll rest
From mundane scandals, his only cares.

I should not wonder, if like the cat
He had nine lives – In every shock
Against decorum I know he sat
More firmly on convention's rock.

Eyes lined with red, a leper's mind
Entrenched beneath the meagre skull,
With crouching hands that have defined
Vicarious joys, and to the full

Pottered obscenely at his own,
Fingering lusts meticulous;
Love's *chiffonnier* in every town,
Old, unabashed, ridiculous.

I heard this cracked harmonica
Vituperate its tunes, that pass
Like spiders of South America
Dart in the dust to kill. The glass

Eye of his soul looked out at me,
Retreated, and seemed to intimate
No good for youth's futurity…
These days are so indelicate!

Allegory

Hear your three symbols of today:
The lamb, the crow, the eagle live,
The crow would bear the lamb away
Fierce-taloned to a falconry;
Gaunt as the eagle he would strive.

The lamb, the crow, the eagle brood
On temporal sorrows; peregrine
Falls to the snare, and I have seen
Raven lamenting in a wood,
And the lone lamb upon the green.

The lamb, the crow, the eagle die;
The lamb must bleed in merciless hands,
The crow decays on shipwrecked sands,
The eagle exiled from his sky –
So did my only eagle die.

Pays Hanté

Green runs the grass there,
In a great wind under the Downs a little after sunset;
Our feet had trod the plain
In other days.
Five tall unknown trees
Austerely watch my feet return alone;
Each night
They watch our ghosts move together again,
They wait as beacons –
Five trees burning,
Dark intensities in a silent land.
I have been far tonight calling the dead,

Calling them through the mist to stand on the old road,
But in the dawn
Came chill resurrection, and I would have slept.

A peacock's wraith stood out upon the path,
And luminous faces with forgotten eyes
Were by me. I, who said,
This year I have no ghosts, new winds have breathed on me
Dispersing dusts – I have no shrouds to consider,
Since passed along the current of my four rivers,
And I am come to harbour.
              Processions touched my hands and said, Return,
The day is with you now –
There stood
Five tall trees, rising in a haunted land.

§

FROM AFAR

From Afar

The fire stirs, creeping afresh from the embers,
Dim is the light, sound died down, faded irretrievably.
I sit thinking of you
Friends, partners of other times…
Gay, lusty, destitute and unsobered:
One hour's delirium
Beating innumerable wings in a web of forgetfulness.
What place is this for such phantasmagoria –
Do you not see I am estranged from you,
Going by new ways, spectator of elemental solitudes?
And on this eve

Now alone at the hearth, a closed book that soon you must be
                                                    forgetting,
Even as I put your memorable gestures from me.

Buddha above the Hearth

God in the shadows hidden, up there above the fire,
Hear me, God, as my heart walks to you, kneels at your clemency –
You have been three days in my house, I know not as yet
If your blessing be shed on the hearth where I would burn rich
                                                    embers for you;
And all my being is a ripe carpet to your feet,
So, delicate may you tread – Answer my long desire
That each hour groweth in me more everlastingly.
I will give no name to my desire, you are master of its flames and ashes;
The winds and the seasons have made it, and nights of ravenous dream –
There is no granting of it till the answer throb in your soul's majesty,
Let a sign be borne unto me from out your immaculate distance –
Take then from my fervour this burden of sighs, prayers and love.

The Caravans Return

The sober
Drenched morning of an October
Haunts me for a moment in the tossing uncertainties of tonight's
                                                    storm;
And I think of the wan daybreaks
That I would have postponed and now acclaim without fear,
Caring nought for the lamentable chime of their past vengeances
                                                    and accusations
Ringing in the white hour of a desolate sunrise –

And at length by my own fire
I unload the delayed caravans of many years:
Though nothing is lost
Much is dulled by forgetfulness, much spoiled with tears;
Now in smooth hours that dread not the freeing of such memories
I will blow on these, that they kindle again in the warmth of the
harvesting.

What If the Bell Is Loud

What if the bell is loud,
Yet call no fervents to the waiting church?
Weary of exhortations
That spring unheard, the preacher tires of faith;
In deserts secretly
The hermit wearies of his solitude.
The wave upon the rock
Beats many a day before the fissure yields.
And when desire is hot
Throbbing within the mind of a creator,
High are the ramparts still
Between it and the outer liberty.
What if a lover cry
Across the autumn glooms in lonely hour
And no voice call again,
No answer come save memory's delicate ghost?
Pity the emptiness
That waits, and all things chilled, grown old with waiting.
Then the world mocks, asserting
Its later creeds, discoveries and lovers.
And will it comfort us,
The image of an old monk in his cell
Penning these lost endeavours
Within the volume of Eternity?

Time Alone Grapples

Wait,
Till it's too late
To draw together the mesh of things half-forgotten?
Past fruit gone rotten,
Decayed in the dry rot of a later season's attic;
Leaves atop of it
And dusts beneath –
God, the very breath
Of these soured love-apples;
The roundworm deals emphatic
Wounds to their resurrection, taking his fill of it.
Time alone grapples
With these vexatious questions,
Making in bonfires
His insolent purifications –
Flamboyant immortalising of our one-time most delicate desires
That have escaped all other fires.

*   *   *   *   *   *

Or shall one start
Hot for certainty – leap into the dark,
Plunge in the chasm
While a cloud
Blows doubting mists around the heart?
Only in such spasm
Set out to clasp and keep
A dream that struggles back to sleep?
I hear the loud
Hurry and disorder of the drums, the bark
Of threatened dangers, the shout of haste…
My fate on the tightrope
Dances, and urges me to dance,
Nor pause, nor hope.
So always goaded recklessly I cast

Unwilling gauntlets at the feet of chance
Challenging waste.
I would have nothing die – yet all the drinking,
Courageous give-and-take of blows, and thinking,
And saying: things once gone, forever lost,
Succours me not, for all is past…
In angry host
I see the hours embark,
And the funnel of my last ship on the horizon sinking.

I Ask No Questionable Understanding

I ask no questionable understanding,
Only
A timely leisure for the disembarkation of thought
From over those cold seas that I would not have calm;
For the still oceans thicken with dumb conceit
As salt lakes petrifying, unthrilled with seasons,
Unadventurous decades
That breed
No come-and-go of days.
Let there be storms,
Elemental ravings to be tried again as before –
Memory's uncountable crosses are set on this horizon
Wary beacons to the graze.
Let there be
New deserts raw and untenanted that thought must traverse,
Weakening,
Wistful with travellers' fears, dismayed – obsessed
With perseverance till the last league is done.
From these trials
And the pursuing of their labyrinths
I would ask everything,
Perchance to distil
One vital hour.

These Rocked the Cradle

I think when I was born
(Under what unknown stars that keep my secret still)
The legendary fates attended me:
Dark whisperings went by
In the corridors whence I sprang,
They clung unseen
Malignantly to the new frail thing –
Chill fates, withering winds already desolating
The paths to be traversed.
Near to the grasp, out of reach, stood the fickle sword
Of crooked courage, backbiting and self-defiant –
A mist of uncertainty
Was my fond nurse, to rock me on her boundless breast;
And the outlaw,
The lurid wanderer of highroads that all children love,
He too was there – Could I have seen
I would have recognised this friend of nowadays
And said:
Clasp me, Adventure!
Seizing the vagabond
By a more kindly mood in that first hour.
All were there,
This life's alarmers, sowing their future harvests,
Rife weeds of conflict –
            all but one
That I name never, Jealousy.

An Exile

Nor fear nor hope had he, only the sigh of patience
Masking emotion; yea the very soul
Was hidden eternally, and backwards crept

The daily longings, the kindled flames of desire
That inward went, to be locked in the ardent cell.
Love moved there warily as a prisoner,
So often baffled in conflict, chill with doubting,
And martyred, fading on his dolorous cross.
He never raised hands to seize and clasp adventure;
But in the silence he would wait for life
To come with beckoning gesture, freeing him
From imposition of memory's stealthy voices.
The wild, the hasty, and the more prodigal,
Even those that judged this nature to be deep,
Paused for a moment pondering, then with shake
Of head went saying: a sombre exile this –
So was there solitude around this man.

You Have Lit the Only Candle

You have lit the only candle in my heart that I am bound to worship,
Kneeling in the draughts of that cold and most solitary place,
Alone, without the stirring priests and breathless sounds of confession
That have made holy such other seclusions, and in their hour of grace
Absolved desires and sins that I am barren of. This sharp
Straight flame of yours is silent, and like a saint throws down on me,
Now I have knelt again after so long on this remembered ground,
The steadfast radiance of his mute impersonality.
You have lit the only candle that shall illumine my wayward paths;
And I tell you, before the time comes when its flames must tremble
                                                        and start,
Facing some great wind of eternity that rends and masters it,
I shall be gone with the thread of its tall spirit safe against my heart.

I Think of You

In the fields
When the first fires of the nightly diamonds are lit,
When the stir of the green corn is smoothed and silent,
And the plover circling at peace like a thought in a dream,
I think of you,
Finger the last words you have added to my rosary.
On a white road
High noon and midsummer witness my love of you
Grown as a firm tree,
Rich, upright, full-hearted, generously spreading
Long shadows on the resting place of our future days.
In a town
I meet many with the thought of you in my heart,
Your smile on my lips,
I greet many
With the love that I have gathered at your fountains,
Drawn from your happy wells
In that far horizon my eyes shall ever see.
I go to the feasts adorned
In a scarlet vestment,
Bejewelled and hung with many trappings –
Under these
Burns the still flame that alone your hands may touch.

I Have Never Loved One
That Was Not Proud at Heart

Not unto him that suffers with proud head
Are given the opiates of forgetfulness.

I have never loved one that was not proud at heart,
So have we suffered in mind's company
And yet alone, each prisoner in a cell.
The ripe, the kernel overripe still in its shell
Fruitful one day after its latent sleep,
Or barren of seed through all eternity –
It matters not, if it so fall, the tree,
Leafless, ungrown, yet broods within the ground
A little flame of its rare entity –
Fire that lives not once out in stormy winds,
Baffled and blown with passions, quenched with sorrow,
Yet burns unquenchable, at peace though mute
Below the tempests in the forest morning.

So May You Nail Your Sorrow to My Name's Cross

That street had no horizon but the rain –
You said your heart was dying, and your life
Chilled with a frenzy that no thought might save,
And dreading your despair I would have gone,
Fled your obscure defeat –
But under the skies
That wept their clouds upon us, this heart-breaking
Might not be stilled, and in the growing night
Dead plaints came from your sorrow. Many a man
Sets hand to ploughing up of memories,
And I have trod the winter streets full oft

Heavy with reminiscence, sorry-hearted:
Yet would it profit us had I then read
Aloud the threadbare list of comfort to you?
Such is no more than wringing of faint hands
Outside the cell of prisoners condemned;
You were the gaoler to your own miseries
For whom no execution waits – Thus thinking
Silent I left you, with no words insincere
That would have chilled us with hypocrisy,
So may you nail your sorrow to my name's cross.

I Shall Depart

There is no end to things; behold the sunset
That sails aloft unseizable and deathless,
Though I may not aspire to that swift chase.
A blind
Cold wind
Blows and is gone again
Far in the distance sighing; his errant pace
Returns in later hour. The bodies slain
In battle climb to heaven on spiritual feet,
Till the earth beckon them again
To come and go on its remembered street.
And never a song
Or thing of passionate adventure falls to dust
Spoiling and faded, when from throbbing heart
Its voice has sprung
In some once-vivid hour.
Of such is fashioned all that I demand
As eager sword to carry in my hand,
So that I fear not on time's battlefields.
                              At most a little rust
Rankles on things that we no longer tend.

But I have closed my door
To those that prate of death, and shall depart
Coursing the firmaments that have no end.

At Fuenterrabia in Spain

God
Loves gold
In his churches –
On these Latin altars are found
Riches that eyes may feast; a sound
Of counted chaplets hesitates – Our cold
Dark aisles breathe other thoughts; we nod
In England, growing old,
Chagrined by Sundays, half-asleep
At the vespers that they keep
There in austerity, as if life were a penance.
I have found
Today such joy in this edge of France,
Such zest in crossing the border
By sea to Spain,

And up the alley meeting
The unknown prospect and the street that winds
Threaded with raucous laughter; the ancient order
Of priests walks here, broidered with silver crosses,
Fresh from a mass.
I saw
A giant haven of gold in a dark church,
The distant altar dominant in the night
Of noon-tide's service –
God loves gold
At his altars brimming;
And here tradition

Burnishes the emblems of a tried religion.
I thought: God smiles
Most distantly at all the muttered prayers,
The true, the would-be fervent,
And accepts
These offerings, gathered by the one that dares
Proclaim a kinship through his priesthood's craft –
God bends
His aureoled head indulgently;
His heart
Is filled with all the things of stress
That we have laid there, in our littleness
At grips with life, putting responsibility
Into the hands of his divinity.
Laughter and tears go to him, and the bold
Gesture of outlaws, the diverse webs we make,
(Weave to unravel later –)
Noise and silence,
The joy in power, the lonely diffidence,
All moods, all tragedies
That flame in red on our lives' histories –
All these go by him on an echoing tide;
Waves passing and broken
They stream to the symbolic light,
Gathered about its token;
We deem it savours eternity…
Yet why should I urge my soul to infinity,
Knowing of old
Its voice must call unanswered here? God will accept
The beggar's sighing and the church's gold.

Cap Du Figuier

I think of the earth sometimes
As a very great ship setting out upon the oceans;
This headland is her prow
And I today's captain, standing at watch where two lands meet,
France and Spain, at this russet island, the full-stop before immensity.
Yet another world's-end; behind me the continent
Gathers its mountains together in the autumn haze.
If the earth be a ship then I am time, and the wings of these white gulls
That pass from wind to wind, are the sole hours that ring in my brain,
While the timeless ocean bears all on the surge of its infinity.

To the Eiffel Tower Restaurant

Espéranto…
The seal on your letter sets me thinking
Of other days and places,
And now I have the past to kneel before my present;
Those old nights of drinking,
Furtive adventures, solitary thinking
At the corner table, sheltered from the faces,
Inopportune invasion of the street.
I feel
Sharp tugs at my memory's sleeve:

The sound of the clock going wrong,
The fleet
Procession of your waiters with their platters –
Drinks held long
In one hand, while the other unwinds a discussion.
I do not grieve

I never grieve
For things gone by,
But all the matter
Of ten years in a childhood's land
That grudges colour to one (save on your tables
Of opulent fruits, trimmed foods, voluminous flowers
That lie most comfortably there waiting our appetite).
I say, all the matter
Of that decade
Comes back to me with your letter.
I feel the mist
Of the room that mocks the fog in the street;
The voices of those of us returned from distant journeys,
They could ring in my ears
From your evocation;
And since from choice
I have abandoned
Those groups that pondered through the night's perspective
Restlessly, talking of foreign towns,
I take this sustenance
From you hand only.
Think how all of France
Divides us now, and the Italian sky
That closes down abruptly on its sunset of six o'clock,
Without lamps in this cold October.
Is England sober,
Clad in its sullen winter moods already,
Or sitting expansively
At the tables in warmed intoxication?
And do you still contemplate
The varying destiny
Of the clients that always must return
To the Tower's beacon, to the Tower's cheer?
Small fry and gros bonnets.

I think the Tower shall go up to heaven
One night in a flame of fire, about eleven.

I always saw our carnal-spiritual home
Blazing upon the sky symbolically...
If ever we go to heaven in a troop
The Tower must be our ladder,
Vertically
Climbing the ether with its swaying group.
God will delight to greet this embassy
Wherein is found no lack
Of wits and glamour, strong wines, new foods, fine looks,
strange-sounding languages of diverse men –
Stulik shall lead the pack
Until its great disintegration, when
God sets us deftly in a new Zodiac.

I Am Not One for Expression

I am not one for expression;
The fish leaps in the stream,
The bird rends the air sharply,
But I linger as if underground
In a web of escaping thoughts.
I have laughed,
Applauded, marvelled, thrilled at others' emotion –
After these what is left in my hand tomorrow but the feel of a
vanished leaf?
(As the sleeper waking from his treasure-dream holds not even a
palm-full of dust.)
You that write,
Having had in your grasp
Men's hearts and words, love, and the earth's intensities –
Even those that boasted of such, upstarts in a penny town,
And the few
That know content, having half-realised
Themselves in a line or two of eternity;

And you to whom all life
Is ripe with fulfilment or dim with unfulfilment,
Now at the end of your fruition –
All of you
Had keys to expression, went up and opened the doors
On glamour, romance, and soul's philosophy;
Set free a running mood,
Put lances in the clutch of your heroes,
Raised them on mountain crests for all to see –
I have no wealth
In the currency of your riches.
I am the pilgrim of lost paths,
The gleaner in the empty harvest field
That others have plucked before I came to it.
Out in the world for a season
I will travel with its pedlars
Learning from them maybe to pick at other trades,
Making a semblance –
Till I sit again, aloof
Like a cross-legged tailor stitching in his small shop,
Handling thoughts that are the ghosts of deeds,
(Ghosts and precursors)
Hammering cold words
On ill-shaped anvils.

To I. T. and T. W. E.

But one or two of us go hand in hand,
You, adolescent, and you the unexpressed
That wear uncertainty upon your breast
Like a flower of many moods, and understand
All things from tasting all the hot wines of life.
We seem so heedless, with only shadows for friends
Along the highway's desert, till fate sends

An unexpected partisan, that the rife
Ranklings of solitude be stilled anew.
You adolescent, the truant to all schools,
Life will not burn, you hold aloft the rules
Of conduct, as you hastily pass through
Those rooms where yet I watch uncertainty
Lifting its torch to light our destiny.

'Les Jeunes'

Tels que de blancs agneaux sagraces ces deux frères
Parcourent le Continent,
Auréolés de feutres noirs, le livre sous le bras,
Leurs rires sont les mêmes.
Toujours blonds et roses ils sément les paroles,
L'un moqueur naïf – l'autre comme un prètre,
Dont le regard fuyant serait la soutane de sa pensée
Pour servir les mots satiriques aux nouvelles ouailles…
Je les ai vu ainsi en maints cafés,
Récolteurs éditant l'esprit – toujours debout,
Tant pressés de leurs nerfs, ils sont à la recherche de la 'jeune France.'

De temps en temps
Un épigramme est serré pour la famille –
Car, là-bas dans le brumes anglaises,
Il y a une soeur qui broie idées d'étrange couleurs,
Trictant son fil poétique
Enchevetré
Dans des rouages de natures mécaniques,
De paysages empaillés,
De spleen pour les gens de province…
Il y a une mère, un père,
(Grand Barberousse) qu'on dit être un avare.

*   *   *   *   *   *

En leur palais de Florence je les vois cherchant querelle aux fleurs;
Disant: douze ballons d'enfant vaudraient mieux près de notre
fontaine –
Et d'une chiquenaude décapitant quelques primevers,
L'un sort pour l'achat d'un verre second-empire dont l'autre se
souvient.

Crepuscule Sentimentale

A lumière d'or sur l'eau…
Elle ne cache rien,
Ou bien
Si tu veux elle
Cache des promesses, des choses jurées
A Dieu.
Trouves-lui un symbole
Et elle existera
En d'autres termes, crée
Par toi en paroles.
Ce n'est que la lumière
De cette taverne, reflétée
Sur les eaux proches et mutables
D'un des canaux de Venise;

Elle demeure
Stable, instable
Après le bateau qui s'élance –
A cette heure
Me vient une nostalgie de la France,
Des feuilles tombées aux boulevards, et des pleurs
Qu'on y a dans une petite ivresse de vin
Couvant les souvenirs, harçelé de 'trop tard'

Qui remettrait toujours,
Toujours le geste sommaire du lendemain –
Mais içi, dans une heure,
Se prépare la vraie nuit
Pour manger, dormir, aimer…
Paris est loin.
Attablé
Je te vois, avec des autres
Aux gestes vifs, aux frêles mains
Qui expriment l'Orient et vantent l'Amérique, venus à Paris
De partout, aux 'Autels de l'Art' –
(Je n'ai jamais connu de Saint
Mais ai vu maints apôtres
Se suivre dans le sentier de leur espoir.)

La lumière se tord sur l'eau,
Ce n'est plus la flamme de l'auberge,
Ne lui donnes pas de symbole –
Ce n'est rien, pas même l'épave
D'un souvenir.
Pleures pour moi ce soir
Avec l'ivresse du vin –
Vas au Boulevard,
Vas à la foire d'automne,
Et sur le tard quand tout se ferme
Je t'aurai vu, grave,
Auréolé de chant de l'avenir.

Opium

Fumerie –
Si j'avais boudé Dieu, ce dieu de l'extrème orient
Que je vois reflété dans les songes que je balançe,
Si je l'avais nargué –
Que d'étranges moqueries
Ne m'aurait-il soufflé au lieu de songe qui me revient
D'une heure très lointaine, finie, outretombe –
Mais je l'ai acceuilli,
Tel les rêveurs qui retrouvent l'amante perdue,
Et la bercent un instant à leur Coeur inassouvi…
Ah fumée,
Un éternal conseil de la destinée,
Vais-je le saisir en votre luminosité souveraine?

Les Masques

J'ai revu tous les yeux des multitudes quittées,
Et le fil de lune triste dans ma chamber au retour
Prés des tulipes écloses en ce printemps féroce –
Lumière d'insomnie, veilleuse palpitante
Qui voyage sans arrêt ou les masques pendent au mur
Et me guettent mollement de leur coin des cieux.
Ils me dirent – Là-bas on vous attend toujours,
Sachant que jamias vous ne nous appartiendrez.

Ce soir, sur les voix russes et les chansons,
Il pleuvait – gotte à goutte les rires s'en allaient
Cherchant un asile dans la foule multicolore;
Les voix déferlaient comme des vagues dans un port
Ou balancent restraintes les naçelles éveillées.
J'étais une barque inconnue, une de celles
Filant parmi les autres, inapperçue,

Muette et sans lumière, qui n'attent aucune brise
Ni le réveil du jour – elle n'a jamais eu d'heure
Exacte ou elle reprend sa destinée.

Les rires s'en allaient, je n'ai pensé à rien
Hors les yeux que je vois et qui ne me regardent plus.
L'aube d'une rue solitaire m'a tenu compagnie,
Et chez moi les masques réveillés, placides, pendus,
Cruçifiés ecstatiques que j'avais aligné,
Pleurent et sourient comme aux temps écoulés.

Ils me voient du même regard quand je découvrais l'aurore
Par leurs yeux inlassables, blémis, incolores,
Sans plaintes et paroles ils sont gais dans le vide –
'Maitre'… diraient-ils – je les préfère au monde entier,
Barques de mes songes, équipages d'aventures
Indéfinissables, inachevés.

Parallax

1925

Parallax

'Many things are known as some are seen, that is by Paralaxis, or at some distance from their true and proper being.'
Sir Thomas Browne

He would have every milestone back of him,
The seas explored, clouds, winds, and stars encompassed,
All separate moods unwrapped, made clear –
Tapping of brains, inquisitive tasting of hearts,
Provisioning of various appetite.
Midnights have heard the wine's philosophy
Spill from glass he holds, defiant tomorrows
Pushed back.
His credo threads
Doubt with belief, questions the ultimate grace
That shall explain, atoning.
A candle drips beside the nocturnal score –
Dawns move along the city's line reflecting,
Stare through his rented casement.

     Earth, earth with consuming breast,
Across its ruined waste, its torturous acre
Draws out his complex fires, drives on his feet
Behind imperious rain, and multiplies
The urges, questions in the wilderness.
All roads that circle back – he shall tread these
And know the mirage in the desert's eyes
The desert's voices wait.
This clouded fool,
This poet-fool must halt in every tavern
Observing the crusty wrecks of aftermath,
Plied by his dual mood – uneasy, still –
Devouring fever of bone transfused to brain,
In that exact alembic burned away,
     Made rare, perpetual.

Come music,
In a clear vernal month
Outside the window sighing in a lane,
With trysts by appletrees –
Moths drift in the room,
Measure with running feet the book he reads.
The month is golden to all ripening seeds;
Long dawns, suspended twilight by a sea
Of slow transition, halting at full ebb;
Midnight, aurora, daytime, all in one key –
The whispering hour before a storm, the treacherous hour
Breaking –
So wake, wind's fever, branches delirious
Against a riven sky.
All houses are too small now,
A thought outgrows a brain –
Open the doors, the skeleton must pass
Into the night.
In rags and dust, haunted, irresolute,
Its passion cuts new furrows athwart the years.

                    Sorrow, my sister –
                         yet who accepts
          At once her tragic hand?
          From pitiless explorations
          Come the unwarrantable deeds,
          The over-proved frustrations.
                    O vulgar lures of a curl!
          Tricks, catches, nimble-fingered ruffian adolescence
          Whose beauty pulls
          The will to fragments –
          Young beauty in a raffish mood,
          Love to be sold,
     Lily and pleasant rose,
     Street lily, alley rose,
     For all Love-to-be-sold, who will not buy?
     Rose, gold – and flush of peach

(Never by the sun formed),
Bloom-dust off gala moon
In restaurants,
Cupid of crimson lamps –
His cassolette
Steams through the coy reiterative tune
Nightlong.
Oh come, this barbed rosette
(Or perhaps spangle
From champagne)
Drops off once out the exit-door –
Or how many thousand prodigal francs
From serious patriarchal banks
Must build the card-house for this 'Grand Armour'?

Sour grapes of reason's vine
Perfecting, hang on that symbolic house,
And passion is a copious mine
No matter how stripped it's always full – carouse
Then, cytherean, with the cursory false love
That has his bed
Gold-lined, and robs you, host that are too fond –
        Cold, cold,
Mind's acid gales arouse the sated old
Fool that was gulled by love and paid his bond –
        Young love is dead.

'I that am seed, root and kernel-stone
Buried in the present, I that exact fulfilment from every hour
Now tell you:
Accept all things, accept – if only to *be aware.*
Understand, no choice is granted,
Nor the prudent craving, nor the ultimate romance –
But the unalterable deed, the mystic and positive
Stands, monumental against the astonished sky
        Of an inquisitive world.
Now fierce, now cold,

Time beats in the hours, threatens from smoky ruins –
And yet to whom the loss
If one be made the sempiternal fool
   Of chance,
Muddied with temporary growth of love's importunate weeds?

   'In the penumbra
   Of the wilderness,
On the rim of the tide along Commercial street
You meet one like you for an hour or two –
But eventual sameness creeps to repossess
All eyes, supplicant, offering unusable fidelities;
Eyes of defiance sulking into assent,
Acute with repetition, aged by a stale demand...
Though I did mark the turn of every hand
In the beginning, tendered my respect
To ante-rooms, while the sand ran from the hours.

   'Think now how friends grow old –
Their diverse brains, hearts, faces, modify;
Each candle wasting at both ends, the sly
Disguise of its treacherous flame...
Am I the same?
Or a vagrant, of other breed, gone further, lost –
I am most surely at the beginning yet.
If so, contemporaries, what have you done?
We chose a different game –
But all have touched the same desires
Receded now to oblivion – as a once-lustrous chain
Hangs in the window of the antiquary,
Dry bric-à-brac, time-dulled,
That the eventual customer must buy...
   (Tomorrow's child)'

      Sunday's bell
   Rings in the street. An old figure
   Grins – (why notice the old,

The scabrous old that creep from night to night
Bringing their poor drama of blenched faces and fearful hands
That beg?)
Two old women drinking on a cellar floor
Huddled, with a beerish look at the scavenging rat –
A fur-collared decrepitude peers
From tattered eyelids
That shrivel malignant before an answering stare –
Old men in the civic chariots
Parade with muffled protestations,
Derelicts spit on the young,
     Oh symbol, symbol,
Indecorous age and cadence of christian bell.

This thin edge of December
Wears out meagrely in the
Cold muds, rains, intolerable nauseas of the street.
Closed doors, where are your keys?
Closed hearts, does your embitteredness endure forever?
Torpidly
Afternoon settles on the town,
     each hour long as a street –
In the rooms
A sombre carpet broods, stagnates beneath deliberate steps:
Here drag a foot, there a foot, drop sighs, look round for nothing,
         shiver.

Sunday creeps in silence
Under suspended smoke,
And curdles defiant in unreal sleep.
The gas-fire puffs, consumes, ticks out its minor chords –
And at the door
I guess the arrested knuckles of the one-time friend,
One foot on the stair delaying, that turns again.

London –
     youth and heart-break
  Growing from ashes.

The war's dirges
Burning, reverberate – burning
Now far away, sea-echoed, now in the sense,
Taste, mind, uneasy quest of what I am –
London, the hideous wall, the jail of what I am,
            With fear nudging and pinching
Keeping each side of me
Down one street and another, lost –
Returned to search through adolescent years
For key, for mark of what was done and said.
Do ghosts alone possess the outworn decade?
Souls fled, bones scattered –
            And still the vigilant past
Crowds, climbs, insinuates its whispering vampire-song:
(No more, oh never, never...)
Are the living ghosts to the dead, or do the dead disclaim
This clutch of hands, the tears cast out to them?
Must one be courteous, halve defunct regrets,
Present oneself as host to 'Yester-year'?

By the Embankment I counted the grey gulls
Nailed to the wind above a distorted tide.
On discreet waters
In Battersea I drifted, acquiescent.
And on the frosted paths of suburbs
At Wimbledon, where the wind veers from the new ice,
Solitary.
In Gravesend rusty funnels rise on the winter noon
From the iron-crane forests, with the tide away from the rank mud.
Kew in chestnut-time, September in Oxford Street
Through the stale hot dust –
And up across the murk to Fitzroy Square
With a lemon blind at one end, and the halfway spire
Attesting God on the right hand of the street –
London –
            Old.
Dry bones turfed over by reiterant seasons,

Dry graves filled in, stifled, built upon with new customs.

Well, instead –
The south, and its enormous days;
Light consuming the sea, and sun-dust on the mountain,
Churn of the harbour, the toiling and loading, unloading
By tideless seas
In a classic land, timeless and hot.
Trees
Bowed to the immemorial Mistral
The evergreens, the pines,
Open their fans –

      Red-barked forest,
       O vast, brown, terrible,
       Silent and calcinated.
       Moonstruck, dewless…
    Or further
    I know a land… red earth, ripe vines and plane-trees,
    A gulf of mournful islands, best from afar.
The sunset's huge surrender
Ripens the dead-sea fruit in decaying saltmarsh.
Then brain sings out to the night muffled thirds,
Resumes the uneasy counting and the planning –

      What wings beat in my ears
The old tattoo of journeys?
Why dreamer, *this* is the dream,
The question's answer. And yet, and yet,
      The foot's impatient (…where?) the eye is not convinced,
      Compares, decides what's gone was better,
      Murmurs about 'lost days'…
      Sit then, look in the deep wells of the sky,
      Compose the past –
         Dry moss, grey stone,
         Hill ruins, grass in ruins
         Without water, and multitudinous
         Tintinnabulation in poplar leaves;

A spendrift dust from desiccated pools,
Spider in draughty husks, snail on the leaf –
Provence, the solstice.
And the days after,
By the showman's travelling houses, the land caravels
Under the poplar – the proud grapes and the burst grape-skins.
Arles in the plain, Miramas after sunset-time
In a ring of lights,
And a pale sky with a sickle-moon.
Thin winds undress the branch, it is October.
And in Les Baux
An old life slips out, patriarch of eleven inhabitants –
'Fatigué' she said, a terse beldam by the latch,
'Il est fatigué, depuis douze ans toujours dans le même coin.'

In Aix, what's remembered of Cézanne?
A house to let (with studio) in a garden.
(Meanwhile, 'help yourself to these ripe figs, *profitez…*
And if it doesn't suit, we, Agence Sextus, will find you another
                                        just as good.')
The years are sewn together with thread of the same story;
Beauty picked in a field, shaped, re-created,
Sold and despatched to distant Municipality –
But in the Master's town
Merely an old waiter, crossly,
'Of course I knew him, he was a dull silent fellow,
Dead now.'
And Beauty walked alone here,
Unpraised, unhindered,
Defiant, of single mind,
And took no rest, and has no epitaph.

What hand shall hold the absolute,
What's beauty?
Silent, the echo points to the ladderless mind
Tumbled with meanings, creeping in foetus thoughts…
(Out, out, clear words!)

Genius is grace, is beauty – shall I be less deceived
Life-long, because of beauty's printed word?
And yet – what's beauty, where?
Perhaps in eyes, those paths,
Quick funnels to the complicated pool
Of the mind. But the thinking eye
Is blank – cold water-veils
Proceed above what sunken curious shells,
What stones, what weed?
The thinker's eye a blank – with flowering words
Back of it waiting, whereas other eyes
Attend to books, bills, schemes, and how-do-you-do's,
Entrench their independence, liberty...
(O liberty that must be so exactly organised!)
   Brain
   Train
   Of conscious passion,
   Music
   Absolution, sweet abnegation
   Of choice – A palm-grove's transmigration
   On soft hawaiian strings
   Softly, to languid ballrooms –
(God grant us appetite for all illusions,
God grant us ever, as now, the sweet delusions).

   Spring flushes the gardens.
In season of return bloom the forgotten days
Thinly; an empty house
   Waits, that has once been mine.
Spring flushes the gardens –
Here a road, there a flowering tree,
And the lonely house
The lost house, the house bereft,
Spider-filled, with the hearth ash-laden from the last fire –
But he that delays here, now an anonymous traveller,
Stares at the evening silence, and without gesture
   Passes on.

The sand is scored with print of unknown feet
Where seas are hollow, tenanted by sound;
The air is empty save where two wings beat
In timeless journeying – deep underground
Brood the eternal things, but in the street
No whisper comes of these, no word is found.
See now these berries dark along the hedge
Hard as black withered blood drawn long ago
Whose sap is frozen dry; a windy sedge
Hides field from ashen field, pale lapwings go
Whining above the heath, and floods are out
Over the meadows clasped in frigid lace
Of wintry avenues, ringed and fenced about –
His life is a place like this, just such a place.
For him no house, but only empty halls
To fill with strangers' voices and short grace
Of passing laughter, while the shadows' lace
Creeps from the fire along dismantled walls,
Uncertain tapestry of altering moods –
Only the sunset's hour, the solitudes
Of sea and sky, the rain come with the spring;
Dark winds that gnarl the olive trees, and moan
Against the shuttered brain that thrills alone
Each night more racked by its adventuring.
The sirens then, beyond the ocean's brim,
Call, and make ready on their ultimate shore,
And singing raise their arms, and wait for him,
Nepenthe rises at the prison door...

　　　　But in what hour, what age
Are siren voices heard across the water?
No – instead
Only bread and rain
Are on the waters –
And in the flooded orient
Dawn
Unwinds from the edge of a gale,

Muffled, old-purple.
Between two hours the dawn runs very surely
Into a morning March.
Wild-fowl from the sedge, thrushes are in the dew
On distant lawns, so you remember...
Is it the end or beginning,
Caesura, knot in the time-thread?
And Paris
Rolls up the monstrous carpet of its nights,
Picks back the specks and forms –
O individual, disparate,
Where now from the river bank?
      From the Seine, up the Quarter, homeward at last to sleep.

– Clothes, old clothes –
      early is it, or noon,
By this alarm clock?
      The rag-man turns the corner –
For him, past one; just *today* here in bed.
So – one begins again?
      so soon preoccupied...
Who's ill, tired, contumacious, sour, forswearing
After last night?
With wine alone one is allowed to think
Less cumbrously, and if one may recall
Little, there's always tomorrow – when a something sore
Gropes in the brain – and shall one not condone
The shame, the doubt of this, the automaton?
      With no particular heartache,
      Only subsiding chords,
      Echoes of transience.

In adolescence creep the first bitter roots
Darkly
To a full rich world –
The rich bitter fullness, where the play stands
Without prompter for the love-scene or the anger-scene.

And... You and I,
Propelled, controlled by need only,
Forced by dark appetites;
Lovers, friends, rivals for a time,
            thinking to choose,
And having chosen, losing.
... 'How long shall we last each other...
            Perhaps a year...
Omens I do not see...'
But now we are three together –
How is it when we three are together
No rancour comes, but only the tired
Acceptance, the heart-ache in each heart-beat?
Full acceptance, beaten out to the very end –
Life blooms against disaster,
            pressing its new immortal shoots against disaster.
And one of us questions, and smiles –
And one of us, smiling, answers with a gesture only –
And one: – 'Ah no – the new cannot put out the old –
Though I clutch on the new I shall not shuffle off the old,
Wrapped, folded together
The new burns, ripens in the known,
Folded, growing together –
Yes – (even to paradox)
Have I not loved you better, loving again?'

Up, down a little world –
            south, north –
            Pale north, dark-hedged; two cities grow and rot there
            Stealthily.
                  War's over, and with it, spring
            That opening blinds let in no more.
                  Only the grey
            Habit of days,
            The yawning visits, the forced revisitations.
            Oh very much the same, these faces and places,
            These meals and conversations,

Custom of being alive, averting of the death-thought.
But in the charnel-cloister Dupuytren,
Down a side-street, there's a full century's matter
Collected –
The death-before-life, the atom in the womb
Preparing – snarled embryos,
                    pinched
By once-roseate poisons.
(Frail brown
Pre-natal dust, what life is it you missed?)
The skeletons swing on a line,
Dark-waxed, patined, defective-boned –
O commemorable fusion of science with disease…
(That was a new contemplation, the death-museum.)
Up and down
On a little track,
With a lighthouse to end the chapter.
The sea is glass – slip briefly into France;
Brown-gold Rhône, slip with me to the other sea
Where the mimosa flowers
Ecstatically for moribunds,
Immensely, in thundering rains.
Time rings in the weakening pulse, aggressive high –
       Time,
              Time –
Do you remember:
A cliff had hidden the wind –
The fishes came, and the gold-eyed plaintive mongrel
To snap at cast-off scraps;
We were talking of mutability –
(Your eyes dark
As a sky when the winter sun wearies of it
Drawing into a cloud.)
       '*Now* at least
We are forgotten of time, this hour escapes him –
              Where he sits
In the workshops

Tying his knots, unravelling,
Spoiling the work of others –
He who dramatizes the nights
Of lovers, and tears fierce words from their insurgent hearts –
He who sits
In the taverns, lusty, aloof,
Condemning, experienced, jealous…
Milord Eternity –'
       And the seas turn mutable foam, in fear transfusing
Themselves to the watcher –
            they have nor wish nor choosing,
But turn, tossing fragments, spars,
Forever – meridian calms
Fill these still classic shores with unaccountable voice,
And in the weeded stones
The carapace life creeps singly, unafraid.

'– Then I was in a train
            in pale clear country –
By Genoa at night,
Where the old palatial banks
Rise out of vanquished swamps
Redundant –
And in San Gimignano's
Towers, where Dante once…
And in the plains, with the mountain's veil
Before me and the waterless rivers of stones –
Siena-brown, with Christ's head on gold,
Pinturicchio's trees on the hill
In the nostalgic damps, when the maremma's underworld
Creeps though at evening.
Defunct Arezzo, Pisa the forgotten –
And in Florence
Benozzo
With his embroidered princely cavalcades;
And Signorelli, the austere passion.
Look – Christ hangs on a sombre mound,

Magdalen dramatic
Proclaims the tortured god; the rest have gone
To a far hill. Very dark it is, soon it will thunder
From that last rim of amaranthine sky.
Life broods at the cross's foot,
Lizard, and campion, star-weeds like Parnassus grass,
And plaited strawberry leaves;
The lizard inspects a skull,
You can foretell the worm between the bones.

(I am alone. Read from this letter
That I have left you and do not intend to return.)

...Then I was walking in the mountains,
And drunk in Cortona, furiously,
With the black wine rough and sour
      from a Tuscan hill;
Drunk and silent between the dwarfs and the cripples
And the military in their intricate capes
Signed with the Italian star.
Eleven shuddered in a fly-blown clock.
     O frustrations, discrepancies,
I had you to myself then!
To count and examine,
Carve, trim, pare – and skewer you with words.
     Words...like the stony rivers
Anguished and dry.
Words clouding, spoiling, getting between one and the mark,
Falsely perpetuating – 'Why he was thus,
Self-painted, a very personal testimony
Of half-expression' – and oh the hypocrisy
Of the surrender in the written word...
(Yet taken from this
The discerning estimate of 'what you've been' –)
What now can be remembered that was seen
Long ago? (always long ago).
The empty seas, the unpeopled landscape, and the sullen acre

Trodden out in revolt –
Associations
Called in unmerited resurrection
Of what's accomplished, dead –
These, and the chasing of the immortal Question,
          The hunted absolute.
                    In the shade of the bitter vine
I sit, instructed fool and phoenix-growth,
Ash-from-my-ash that made me, that I made
Myself in the folded curve of Origin –
Heredities disclaim, will not explain
All prior mischiefs in the bone, the brain –
          Only a ponderous mirror holds
The eyes that look deep and see but the eyes again.

One for another
          I have changed my prisons;
Held fast, as the flame stands, locked in the prism –
And at one end I see
Beauty of other times, mirage of old beauty
Down a long road, clear of the strands and patches of
associations,
Keen, resurrected, very clear –
– And at one side
The symbol of the vacant crossroads,
Then the veiled figure waiting at the crossroads
Leaning against the wind, urging, delaying…
(I have come for you, Peer!)
– And behind me
The candles of thoughtful nights,
And the green months, solitary,
Across dividing seas –
And again behind me, the cities
Rising on the inexpressible meaning of their streets,
Unaltering – and the eyes lifting over a wine glass,
Holding the inexpressible, playing terror against acceptance –
Eyes, and siren voices lost at dawn…

Only the empty dawn
Comes, over the harbour; with the getting-back to day,
The resumed love-songs and the rhythms of illusion.
– And around me
Legend of other times on dry gold background,
Pitted with slow insinuations
Probings of now defunct animalculae...
Worm, mighty and dead, established in the paint and the
tapestries,
Having ended your statements.
Only the statement, the unalterable deed only
Stands, and is no more than a halt on the track –
– And at last, before me
In fierce rise and fall of impetuous seasons,
The articulate skeleton
In clothes grown one with the frame,
At the finger-post waiting, aureoled with lamentations.
'Hail partner, that went as I
In towns, in wastes – I, shadow,
Meet with you – I that have walked with recording eyes
Through a rich bitter world, and seen
The heart close with the brain, the brain crossed by the heart –
   I that have made, seeing all,
   Nothing, and nothing kept, nor understood
   Of the empty hands, the hands impotent through
         time that lift and fall

   Along a question –
   Nor of passing and re-passing
By the twin affirmations of never and forever,
   In doubt, in shame, in silence.'

from
Poems Two 1925
1930

Simultaneous

At one time
The bottle-hyacinths under Orvieto –
At one time
A letter a letter and a letter –
At one time, sleepless,
Through rain the nightingale sang from the river island –
At one time, Montparnasse,
And all night's gloss,
Splendour of shadow on shadow,
With the exact flower
Of the liqueur glass in its glass.
    Time runs,
        But thought (or what?) comes
Seated between these damaged table-tops,
Sense of what zones, what simultaneous time-sense?

    …Then in Ravenna
The dust is turned to dew
By moonlight, and the exact
Splayed ox-feet sleep that dragged the sugar-beet
To dry maremmas
        Past Sant' Apollinare,
          Fuori Mura.

    In Calais Roads
The foam-quilt sags and swells,
Exact are the land's beacons to the sea –
Twin arms crossed, thrown across sleep and a night-wind.
Time falls from unseen bells
On Calais quays (that were sometimes a heart's keys).

    Red bryony
Steeps in loose night-air, swelling –
October crumples the hedge –
Or the wind's in the ash, opening the seed-pods.

(The revolution in the weeds –
Rain somewhere. Rain suggests
Their dissolution to the seeds.)

Midnight,
While some protect their trades
Forcing the line – sleep takes them.
But the baker
Cools at the sill, yeast raising auburn flour.

Midnight,
And trains perambulate (*o noctis equi*);
Faust is in hell that would have stopped the horses of night
In their gallops, that would have galloped atop of them,
But was outpaced, overthrown for too exact questioning.

And in Albi
Les orguilleux sus des roues continuellement
                              (hell's fading fresco),
And in Torcello
The mud-fogs now, and on all unknown
Ripe watery wastes
the rich dead silence.

Silence – or a night-wind on a lawn
Turning the pages one by one of a forgotten book.

In Provins

So he ran out knocking down the brigadier –
Mince alors: said the officers to each other
In the hotel at the end of the Sunday meal, *fumant la pipe*.

　　　And rain ran in new ditches
Beating on sooty walls where the ramparts are falling
In Provins, ville-haute – with the gale up the winter's watery veins
In clipped crooked fields – wind in the nerves of winter
(The black branches) – in the streets' draughty funnels.

Next morning the lieutenants cantered out in clear sunlight
Past the Jardin Public, a place of shallow waters rising.
What is left of old carvings… seamed fragments in an odour of
　　　　　　　　　　　　　　　　　　　　　　violets,
And from a café crept the unexplained scent of frezias.
Sun descends on the streams, travelling down the green water.
Against écarlate de Gand and bleu de Nicole they matched their
　　　　　　　　　　　　　　　　　　ners, noir de Provins,
Famous cloth, fast-dyed in the Durteint, hard river-water.
And Abelard
In these level meadows for two years was teaching.
And Thibaut leaned
From the high-town over a murmuring valley,
Thibaut, lord and love-singer who ordered the walls and a
　　　　　　　　　　　　　　　　　　　　　monastery.
Word and gesture all one now, dispersed by the unrecording wind,
Other footsteps now, patterning the soundless mould.

Dome on the sunset, blue dome on high hill-distance
Where the ramparts are falling – only a Caesar's tower
Catches the wind still and the rain's minute deteriorations.
The moon collects on puddle-water –
Lilac and prune-flush, suffusions then shadows of nightfall,
Wing-rustle in quickset… and suddenly that hunting-music,
Delaying chords of horns, suspended chords
After silence.

All day I have had memories coming back at me with their
gesture of meetings and partings,
And the sense of some moment in this place that is a memory to be.

By the roadside, what's past... Then the *now* with its hotel
                                                    bedroom
Where one traveller replaces another – one traveller the
                                        abstraction of all –
Time's seasons or shadows put forward, remembered in the
                                                wallpaper –
Sad spring still frigid, summer with flies, then the harvests
                                        beyond the octroi,
And the long sheet of winter wrinkled and knotted with branches...

After the soldiers...shuffle and stamp in the clotted sawdust...
                                        the commercial gentry:
'Splendeurs et Misères'? Mais mon vieux, tu n'es pas de ton temps!

from

Relève into Maquis

1944

Relève into Maquis

The mayors put up the Order on the walls:
'Labour, well paid, in Germany today.'
Laval found better with these words: '*France calls*
All men of France... Each man who goes will free
One prisoner... Duty... Brothers ... Gratitude ...'
Three generations looked at it, and said:
'Grandfather, father, self – we fought the Boches
Each in his youth, then prime – shall yet, today.
It's NO. The Relève, this "changing of the guard"
Is planned for dupes, by Vichy's fear of us;
They want a France unmanned. We shall not go.'

And a mean wind blew doubt – 'Can one claim a son?
If so one takes his place.' But no. Meanwhile
A million and a quarter prisoners stay in the Reich,
In France come hunger and threats between nerve and flesh;
In July of '42 the first prisoner-train,
The barter of the Relève: three hundred, packed
Like a load of curses, sick, and half un-limbed.

Man sits in a fireless kitchen head in hands,
'From under our feet the ground... and France is done...
Is done? Is *down*. But I live. I'll fight against that.'
Just before dawn he unearthed the rabbit gun
And his old revolver, blessed by Spain, and went –
To the high lands by the goat track, a wind of decision
Blowing dawn into day. 'Wife and life now these two...'
Gun and pistol under knee after the four-hour trek he sat
Till a boy surged calling 'Password?' 'Not a hundred miles from
                                                            Vichy'
'Nor a hundred months from freedom.' So into Maquis,
Hidden camp of partisans, francs-tireurs, guerrillas –
'Refractories to law and order' Vichy calls them;
Into the Secret Army the months have made them.

They swore him in: Enlisted until war's end –
Not to see folks or friends again – Don't count on any pay –
Death if your weapon's lost – Total secrecy, death if not –
Tolerance of each man's views, religious, political – and
Obedience to Maquis discipline in its very hard totality.
Marseille, Lorraine, Angoulême, Lille, Savoie, Franche-Comté,
Paris, Bretagne, Languedoc, Normandie – here is all France.
Loam and letters, student, shepherd, mason, agronomist,
Army-captain, priest, mechanic, and a lawyer-poet. Today comes
                                                         a veteran
Of Spain and of the other two wars each side of that.

As yet there's a gun for every twentieth man –

'Always you hold your hand till the strategy's ripe.
You time your fuse for success. You hold your hand
Till it finds Death's hand responding as an ally.
This is the start. When we have won we shall build
              Not out of *hope*, but out of *strength*,
                    Freedom – signed, FRANCE.'

Man Ship Tank Gun Plane
1944

Man Ship Tank Gun Plane

To Edward Thompson

GUNS far away – then last, closest. And ring-wise or splayed out?
    Like London
Arc, 50 by 30. At night. How uncharted the problem of sound,
Though the middle-ear's filter salutes, comes up at the double to
    solve,
Hurt most by a break in the scurry, by the pause that resembles a
    wound.

No thing is confused; all's in order. Time noted. Last *lares penates*
    Pressed finally after long years in small bag on the couch
    wait the hand,
Ready for 'smartly'... 'fare onward'. So, pacing, sireenly...
    (O sister,
You turned one, telling the Yanks "'alf a blitz 'alf a mo' on the
    Strand)...
Come *mine*, mine-mine... mine, between 10 and 10.1, the
    all-closest (guns I mean)
And the heart of it nears, yes? It does. It breaks up and the
    pattern is lost,
Lost, no, but scattered, forked-out now; ah look, the sound cedes
    it to vision –
Have we storm? We have storm... *peak*, maybe – (keep it
    patterned whatever the cost),

Storm-at-sea... Round this Horn yet... All's relative...
    Mount, climax, then decrescendo...
Peak – only fools wave-count – it's *peak* counts, thrust up
    through this giant tattoo...
Percentage of average... 8 million... *but for soldiers in battle,*
    this, always,
Who say: 'If your name's not on it why then it is never for you.'

Rage rave in your high loft majestic – for look, now the wild
    horses have it
Burst loose in the dizzy skies in their crazy mad gallopade,
Rearing-careering – like planes, yes... can hear them – and
    roaring-careening,
Part-sound, part-vision, part-sensed – planes sniped in an air
    enfilade.

So! Down-come of satellite steels, cascade of the shrapnel olives,
Casual flora of lead bloomed on street, iron spawn from the sky's
    black breast,
The up-gash of incandescence, and crystalline chandelier
Christmassing down from 12,000 (the purpose amidst the feast).
I told you: sound yields it to vision – Then the guns, flares, glass,
    crash, tracers
Condense of a sudden on '*There?*' Do the flames sit in west or
    east?
More like in the south – no, Soho – somewhere back of the plays
    and Eros,
(*Superb* is the fireman's skill)... And what now? The whole night's
    at rest.

I know – you hate these things written – wanting bluebell
    a-quiver in heather,
The secular flight of lone heron in lieu of massed iron wing,
Seeking olive at peace in grey stone-land, and glint on wild fur
    and feather
From sunrise and sunset, and ruins where only the *long*-dead
    sing.

Bat into seagull, welcome! Delft on its old shelf safely,
With only for trepidations those of the sewing machine;
Turn fresco of flames into tide-piece, match gull's wing with
    stone-white on Downland,
Some time hence scarred turf will renew battle-slough revert to
    March green.

Some time hence they will come, I suppose, mood and time to
    weigh and consider
What metre best fits what matter... If the Love-Courts were just
    in their day...
Man will study old specious disputes, things like 'the sex of
    angels'...
Some, turn to the pink in a flint, and the artisan's osier way.

*   *   *   *   *   *

But NOW, no. None of such. All's at war. In front of me sea, and
    it's FRANCE;
And beyond that, the past, and it's SPAIN. Death hurls down a
    comrade's lyre:
Mid-March it is Alun Lewis, death precedes him with Nordhal
    Grieg;
The whole face of one dream is SMOKE, and the voice in the
    next shouts FIRE
Loud, loud, in the ear. Long, terrible, gaunt the enforcement of
    waiting –
Does the wind from above blow chill, is there sign to vouchsafe
    us a date?
Here day after week and month after year, an in vassalled
    countries,
Man burns: 'It is I, one being, but I in my millions, *I wait,*

And... nought?' Nought, nought, and nought, *nothing* –
    impeccable Nothing.
Round as the total circle with zero at full in the midst,
Hinged to invisible vacuum, suspended in seasonless ether,
Greater than unlaned ocean, static, no 'last' nor 'first'

In its nature, like Time. Like Time? Ah! But Time is live too, is
    imperfect,
Subject to change, has springs, and when they are darkly pressed
UP, peoples! haste history; come, dictators and traitors, to trial –
Convulsed are the panoramas, and see, when they fall to rest

Cuts through the dust-cloud THE TRUTH, as spare and white
    as pure bone is.
All must march in appointed order: Man flies across the West,
Man triumphs on in the East; when the South is dynamited
The North skirls down convergent – so must it come at last.

Dèpart à zéro. *Our* say. The fifth spring. The initial and ultimate
Surge, that the feet have learned and the years have stored up –
    till it come
With its roar and tornado, its science, its vigour, its fury, its lava,
At last, like a mistral-boreal – CHARGE – sure as the African
    drum.

THEN, YES – to the arts of peace, to their modes and themes
    and values,
When the armies have battled through, and the dragons' teeth
    have sprung
Sown wide by the conscript millions exiled in teuton death-land,
And the worker clasps the soldier, and the *Marseillaise* has swung

Freedom into fulfilment. Then yes, to a measure of heart's ease,
In a room at The Rising Sun, with a drink to all races' increase –
The landscape no longer khakied, the man on the rick with the
    hayfork,
And the tank led out with the horse to furrow – Piers Plowman
    at peace.

from the
Bodleian Manuscript

Love's Alba Against Time, Time's Against Love

Time counts the lovers' strokes,
Each, stringing his knots along endeavour.
Devil – what have I to say to thee?
Wij beminnen elkander...
    we love, love, we love on, in dutch, so.
Who *says* unsays much later;
Who *all* unsays has all said once.
O n c e ? Is that treachery or is it time?

De fil en aiguille, au fil de l'heure...
Filles et fils de l'heure, écoutez:
'Il y eut une fois'... Ay, that's my enemy,
'Once a time', 'ago',
And as Aragon as it
'Aima, ai-ma' –
You need no other histories.

So in the blue room
What's mine's yours, ours, in fief hilden
For that himself Time is;
So it's not 'you and I', it's Time's sport...

Time's foe, my friend,
Gin, the white king –
In his ermines lives possibility,
His card-houses are my Spanish castles
To which the thread of Ariadne is
    What will have been.

Time like a Mexican, a mask on a desert;
The desert full of sacrificial round-stones well-blooded,
Not seen, sensed only, tenants of the long unfinished poem –
Better a stroph or two in honour of the white king:
Oh gin, white king... oh what a lordly lover...
Making much of nothing... wrap oh wrap me into your ermines...

And here's your shaving-water and your shoe-trees,
Braces and pommatum and your watch and key chains,
Also nine o'clock, sir, all safe sir –
       but not your lover, sir –

Love, Death, Time, Weather

                  so's your Englishman –
O go-for-a-sailor as it's peace-time,
And shatter the context of the blue-red-white.
Say, do they touch at Colon, do they fetch up in the Toulon
Darse?
They do, they swing about – and it's up to you.
After so many other afters is there no now?

But I don't think the Poste Restante
Changes our inner geographies nor yet heals hearts,
Much, nor yet do time's heels
Properly leaden heart's spring buds under, nor now nor finally.
Man, your brief uncoiled ache flips back into place like a curl.
 – Three, four… will my love come?
Late late, on morning's wings
A-mourning what's got, not held.
What's held?
That hand on the bed-cover, that's surely a finality,
In visible focus, punkt –
Held, or for later? (such things have been).

Had I no love I'd a-many,
I'm wrongly angrooved –
Eve and I of myself, how did I come to live in this place?
Shifting zones of the centre!

(But the north-wings calmly nebulate round the Philippine
                                                          rice-gods –
This stamp to what collector?)

Between Time and Etc

Living in the past and the future
I see barrages and heart-breakings,
Sameness running by sameness, defied by difference,
Difference overcome, etc.

ETC's large, is omnipresent;
The coming and going of ETC (new god).
What to think – and to whom hand it?
Yet Time is hardly ETC;
Through with time soon, on with ETC.

We depend on a word
... Dijon... Gueret... for our thought-lines, our Marches and
                                                  summers.
On 'Aima, or how-would-it-have-been granted certain
                                                  considerations?'
On 'I lay in a field and thought to go further',
On 'the perfect sonnet',
On 'death November 6' – and deaths that are to be.
For before all 'a synchronous comprehension of things' is it not?
One hand on the telephone, one opening, say, a bill,
When the fact of each death first...
No need for pondering what you know and they must guess,
The gaps between, ghost-lines.

All of it so much one thing and another –
So in Venice
That repository of old ships
And the fan-bridge – if you linger by dates.
Everywhere the
Ephemeridae of nights, alone and not alone.
Beginning with Dowson, then 'in Timon's rage',
Having it out with love and time...
Are we the real?
Started out of utmost improbability,

Putting it mainly between asterisks, falling into metres,
In a time of waiting (dost ever know any other time?)
I knew the apparent sweet and sharp of the lives of others,
Such obstinate credos as wave on wave,
The never samely repeated BLANK of each spring –

O landscape of the green field, gin bottle and intention,
Next year's hot foot with his 'As you were!'

Tell It, Glen

They lie, all those who say 'The world is beautiful
Because it holds all things and time runs still
Over the crowns and corpses, both are one to him,
Sorrow and joy are one, for no man has his will.'

They lie, such times they say 'We cannot bring
Disharmonies to concord, wars must be
Part of our progress, growth, machinery,
Strengthening our manhood, as one lops a tree.'

They lie, who say 'Look for it to the sky,
Your happiness, life is a swathe of pain.'
They fail, who fashion then an ivory tower
With pride of despair or shuttering-in of brain.

Hast ever seen one climb an ivory tower
That has to work at filling every hour
With speed-up goods? And in the hours between
Shuffles his thoughts with heavy footsteps where
The sudden earth's a soft or sullen green
By pathways to the pits, where that first flower,
When flowers come, seems half a bitterness,
Almost an idler's jibe – For who can use

Such a joy who must be counting: shoes,
Miles, wages, dole, cuts, lay-off, mother's face:
'Go back tomorrow, son' – and at that place
Pass this untroubled bud of liberty...
Did 'God' make man? Woman and man made me;
'God' must have made the flowers, for they are free;
Not I.

A living poet tells of one long dead,
A footloose singer came on spring's first flower,
So blue it brought him tears for her who'd lain
Her body by another's in that year,
That once was his, no longer now – He said
Merely: 'It was so blue, it was herself again.'

We do not weep for love: we call for life,
 – Let love come if it will – for meat and bread,
Man's due and common rights; yes, and time to be
Aware of being alive before we're dead.

Down in those mines under the sea itself.
Do you know what we look like, people, at twenty-three,
Some of us? Hollow-faced, ashen, sombre and scarred,
Lop-sided, shuffling, tooth-rotted – people, that's me.

Glen is my name, Northumberland – out of work.
I did the Hunger March in thirty-four.
Now sit and think: no job. The dole drips pence.
Do I conclude: 'Life's this' or 'Is there more?'

And Also Faustus

Faust longed for a new world
And got it –
Ran through the transmogrifications of the pure intellect, its
                                    philosophies and appetites,
And came to the end of it.
Come, death, take me – quoth. Or was it the mercenary old deil's
                                    contract that called 'time'?
Whichever, it's a despair-story.

What do you think, would Faustus have gotten it clear *now*?
Hitler would have destroyed him 'with honours':
'Powerful man that…Make it a resounding example…'
He couldn't have enregimented Doctor Faustus.

What do you think, would the Doctor have come down into the
                                    street,
As we say in France,
Preluded with laughter the vacillations of the bewildered
                                    intellectuals
(As no doubt he does now)
And set them his teasers?

Yet the Doctor could be claimed as the highest of the honourable
                                    ivory towers,
Gone in the head with too much study in the chase of the
                                    absolute…
(Claim him, thus will you never hold him.)

I think the Doctor would have come down into the street
In his black velvets with a touch of red at the throat
And fallen in step somewhere between the old seared comrades
                                    and the young.

You wouldn't have heard him sing but it's he would have swung
                                    the singing,

You mightn't have seen him, that ageless and timeless, but very
much there,
The kind that deflects a bullet-on-the-way from its mark.
They can't kill him anyway, and what he means…
How often History is a cruel march; how easily the desert
becomes a cataclysm –
How often this year I think: Les morts et Faust avec nous.

Yes, It Is Spain

What is a bomb?
Something I can't yet believe.
What is a tomb?
Something I can't yet see.
And what is a wound in its wounding,
And the shot cutting a vein and the blood coming
Out of an eye, say, stabbed – are these things too for me?

Bitter, how bitter, do you remember in a certain by-now long ago,
Anger boiling through in tears on the foul London midnight stain.
18, 18, 18 – if a man, yes, I'd have been shifted over into it then,
Into the great-to-do, the last one, the Grande Guerre,

With some cross-eyed crossroad finger pointing at me
'On!' on to some bottomless pit for the long waiting and wondering:
'Can you tell me what it's about?' till the hour's coming
With its 'Ready for death?' 'Hell no – ready for nothing'… that's me.

You, man, mumbling that misplaced, ridiculous 'a spot of bother',
O brother contemporary, and some of you the salt of the earth –
What else could you do but go? We shall not forget you,
(And that's a fact, humanly not officially said),
Not forgive the present Flanders-Poppy flaunting ahead towards
the next one,
By La-Der-des-Ders into La Prochaine. I have not forgot my dead.

You think this is something new? No; this too becomes Spain,
All of it, all of it's Spain, with the dial set at Revenge –
No past pageantry of wan mothers and lovers weeping,
Ruined, undone for ever, that Spain cannot avenge.

I'm of a mood tonight, boy, marked DO NOT TOUCH,
Though somebody, say, like Villon, may have the best of it,
Long dead and safe from the shells and cries and wounds,
And the scythes of war mowing ground for our latter-day tombs.

I'm of a mood with Bosch and Zola and Villon,
Who brooked no nonsense, who wrote and painted and said
Their NO against foolery, NO against lying, their NO to
The proud-fleshed fakir, their NO to the living-dead,

The popes and imposters, the critics pragmatic, the pomps – to
Prick irony into function by use of the heart and the fact –
Into the washtub with History, for the better showing of it;
Then, now, à la mode du temps – that the artist becomes the act.

Blake too – you'll do well to remember that naked man's
                                                    announcement:
'It is impossible, yes, for truth to be told *so's understood*
And not be believed'. Great Blake is the Day of Judgement,
Vengeful, oppressive, peculiar – Blake's all to the good.

Daddy Hogarth, and Faust, Shakespeare, Chaucer and Marlowe,
Goya, Heine and Daumier, and the long-exiled giant, Hugo,
Dante – what do you think they'd say to you, artist in hesitations?
Shall I call on these our dead for their answer? 'Go,

Learn from the day's ruins and tombs' they say, 'our trust's in the
                                                                people
Who fought against iron, Church and Bank, with naked fist,
                                                    fight not in vain –
Every man to his battle, child; this is yours, understand it,
In that desert where blood replaces water – Yes, it is Spain.'

To Eat Today

In Barcelona today's
air-raid came as we were
sitting down to lunch after
reading Hitler's speech
in Nuremberg. The Press.

They come without siren-song or any ushering
Over the usual street of man's middle day;
Come unbelievably, abstract, beyond human vision,
Codicils, dashes along the great maniac speech –
'Helmeted Nüremberg nothing', said the people of Barcelona,
The people of Spain – *'ya sabemos*, we have suffered all.'

You heroes of Nazi stamp, you sirs in the ether,
Sons of Romulus, Wotan – is the mark worth the bomb?
What was in it? salt, and a half-pint of olive,
Nothing else but the woman, she treasured it terribly,
Oil for the day folks would come, refugees from Levante,
Maybe with greens... one round meal... but you killed her,
Killed four children outside, with the house, and the pregnant cat.
Hail, hand of Rome, you passed – and that is all.

I wonder – do you eat before you do these things,
Is it a cocktail or is it a pousse-café?
Are you sitting at mess now saying 'Visibility, medium.
We got the port or near it with half a dozen', I wonder –
Or highing it yet on the home-run to Mallorca,
Cold at 10,000 up, cursing a jammed release...
'Give it 'em, *puta Madonna*, here, over Arenys –
Per Bacco, it's nearly two – bloody sandwich it's made down there –
Aren't we going to eat today, *teniente*? Te-niente?'
Driver in the clouds fuming, fumbler unstrapping death.
You passed; hate traffics on; then the shadows fall.

On the simple earth
Five mouths less to feed tonight in Barcelona.
On the simple earth
Men trampling and raving on an edge of fear.
Another country arming, another and another behind it –
Europe's nerve strung like catapult, the cataclysm roaring and
                                                                        swelling...
But in Spain no. Perhaps and Tomorrow – in Spain it is HERE.

Pamiatnik – Memorial of Bittersweet

This is the place
Of indescribable expression, like the look on the face of a certain
                                                                        morning.
This is the house
Where so much of much, so much of nothing happens.
This is the day
And the night
And the dawn
And the tear
Coming out of the wine or the heart temporarily sterile.
This is the place of near-despair, the crucible of world-sorrows.
This is the place
Of the news-letter bleeding out a lynching;
Cell of ferocity, seam of defeat, zone of continuation.
This is the place of Spain-my-Spain –
These agonies, laced with individual sorrows.

This is the house of time withering away,
And time running, and time at a loss,
Like a foot forever on the stair, and the return of dying called
                                                                        winter.
It is no place of linked easy lovers;
Its temper is bittersweet, its pulse is called poetry,

Its heart is a roaring red, its conscience intransigent.
(O it can be soft and sweet too – how long how long, my darling?)
Here often sits December, with the wan drip of the month
Giving the blackout, when the peasants play at Brueghel on the roads.
It can hate and love and scorn in one, it is cruel;
It is a roaring red, I said, under its proud-necked sufficiency.
It sits in judgement on the creeping and racing of the century
Under the warring flags of victories and assassinations
And the waves rising and rising
Of the wrath of outraged humanity –
Judges, and fiercely finds wanting.

There is nothing we can do for it, nothing, oh nothing;
It hates us, it hates us, it hates us –
It is like me,
It is like life.

E O S

Come spring there might be armistice
Between half-loving warring two –
Can truth evolve from travesty?
I think our first's our last solstice.

He will he will not, both – which most?
All-inconsistent, true to plan;
Take it or leave it while you may –
This is a three-in-the-morning man.

Between the book and bottle move,
The poltergeist is at the bar;
A 'portrait of the man I love?'
Oh hound that bays an icy star.

Aurora boreal was our sign,
The red in the night explaining fear,
The drunken burn, the knife in the air,
The pashing mire and January wine.

Lie in this bed while yet you may,
Get you your most and I will mine;
To kill and to remake each day,
Such was part-lesson of the vine.

Kiss that holds out how should a tear?
Without the wave there is no strand.
What be these siltings in your earth,
This foreign body in my land...

What price the candle, what, the prize?
Act 1 – and last. The month has gone
Wasting fine substance every day;
We talk, we doubt; the hackles rise.

Meanwhile all fate climbs to the roof
Watching the iron cars grind on
And echoes: Heil. The Vienna strings
Are snapped, the iron chord bears down.

So died one land, while private spate
Of scorn and sweet ran hot and chill,
The spring of 1938
Marched, and the omens boded ill.

Sophisticate of simple man,
All's one; fate nears with drilling feet –
Oh shambles shambles of the heart,
'How fares in there? The world's in it'.

The world, cross-currented, a-glow,
Identified that while with you...
We ate our lotus there a month –
'No other taste shall change this...' *No?*

No other taste? Deliverer time
Writhes in the bud and waits the spring.
But lovers' bird a phoenix is,
Half-crazed with hope; on dazzling wing

It rides the flurry of the Horn –
Think you we'll round those furious tides?
The look-out man still calls: She rides!
Hush on his daring until port.

When's that, and where – Volubilis?
How comes to me a name like this,
Lure with same nothing at the end,
Stage on the road I-hit-I-miss?

*   *   *   *   *   *

Volubilis stands yet on sand
In Africa with its Roman twist
That time wrecked too, that death has kissed –

Ay, that's the lotus never-land.

Sequences from a Long Epic on Spain

1

It begins in Morocco, under the long-depressed Crescent,
With a voice in the night: 'Turn out! Manoeuvres!'
And the Moors took
The usual dawn-roads and then – it all got different.
'Had we but known…for there are paths between the Moroccos;
We could have fled, but we did not know.'
Ordered into planes, this, German, that, Italian,
Moors into Spain marched, gun at rib, wondering;
And came
'Into lands of Spain, si señor, us, *Regulares*.
They told us then: 'Fair in Seville; you, Guard of Honour'.
The devil a fair! But threats, blows and secrecy incomprehensible;
A train, a train *and* a train, and no place with a name, for us.
Then in two weeks
Crashed doubt into truth: WAR. But *whose* war? Now we know.
We are not prisoners. We are deserters to the Republic;
Walked from that place of many arches (Segovia), a woman
                                        showed us the way.'
Oh Moors of earnest word – you five I saw later in Madrid.

2

It begins, for me, in a Montmarte street with a crazy footstep
Racing, pleading, at midnight: 'I *must* talk to someone, you…
Listen, woman: if you know how close it is,
The horror…Can you stop it? I am an airman; I fell.
It is not that. They'll use me tomorrow again,
And I'll go wherever it be; I'm a commercial flier.
That is not it.
I saw my brother burn in the sky; I was a child,
Near Verdun, near Verdun – 1918.
Planes fall, burning. I know hell. Do you know hell?
And not it's coming again…

If you knew, if you knew – so soon – or do you know?

> Gone with the wind of Ethiopia-laden July,
> A scar of a man. What was it, foreknowledge, coincidence?
> And then, in four days, in a roar of flames it began.

19   ------   Barcelona   -------   19,   immortal July.

Madrid 1936

I cannot see the landscape for the tears,
But winter has come with snow in the new craters there.
They have died and died in Madrid, perhaps mainly the children;
Look at their pictures, peoples, observe the virtuosity
Of death, the pock-signer, the master in fanciful sameness –
Behold this singular leprosy,
This hither-and-yon of destruction that needs no one *wound*;
The children's mouths are open in death,
Is it suspense? No, a finality.
What is the answer to come?
PEOPLES, WHAT IS YOUR ANSWER?

It is winter in the round still parks,
Snow and misery are the temporary new crutches of death –
Only, over the snow fly the words of all Europe now…
Words from the Pacific Americas, words of Antillean temper,
Coming together, comrades – words from Finland to Abyssinia;
The scale fills in, the octave is complete.
They are all here
For Paco, with Paco the espadrilled, once the hod-carrier, now
                                        Spain's Red Army man.
Words of men, deeds of men – men here and coming,
Grain cast out of the great seed-bag of man's heart,
Ready seed sown, fallen, moving, risen and proven.
This is the International, Paco – this too is a finality.

December 1936, Madrid

By the Manzanares,
And the Parque del Oeste and the Casa del Campo,
By the Puetra de Hierro and the Hill of the Partridges,
University City... Casa de las Flores... Quixote and Pancha in
                                                    the snow,
(Their statue a front now)...Carabanchél...
By the shards of the southern wasteland,... Arguélles,. Vallécas,
Líria's Palace in rivers of flame...
By the Puente de los Franceses, by the Southern Station,
Cuatro Caminos, Tetuán (the air bursting with death)...
By Úsera, Araváca, Garabítas,
by Las Véntas, Monclóa, Lavapiés,

B a t t l e.

If the poets be not dead – but what matter if the poets be dead –
Nothing matters but Madrid in its winter of death and dying –
Yet the poets were not dead; they came, anguished, wondering,
                                                    and erect
Men of Madrid and women, and children on road and street
Taught what a clenched fist means when what is in it is truth.

*   *   *   *   *   *

– Things in the sky, things broken, hunger afoot ever earlier,
                              how many statues in twain?
I cannot compute the bodies, cannot compass the dead.
    And one day
                    Came from the sky this, a present to the earth:

Journalist's despatch, November something: 'Witnessed today
opening of box dropped over Madrid by parachute of Francoist
plane. Contents, horribly mutilated body. Carved-up corpse of
Republican aviator. Obviously work of professional butcher.
Note attached: "We will serve all your fliers in like manner."'

His name was Juan Antonio Galarza.

December 1937, Madrid

They did not pass – through Toledo Gate where only the sunset
passes,

(I have seen I have seen)
With the final *Bmmmmm-p* of hand grenades, beholding the
smoky battle.

'Not for us, those', said the sentry there. 'Now tell us of Major
Attlee

Who came here a week ago. Is he true? If so, what will he do for
us?'

...And the smoky battle,

Smudged, an uncertain fresco; how far – a mile? Less than two,
Under Madrid in the snow and gold of December.
Florída, Gran Vía, Telefónica,
Street of Shells, pride of edifices;
Noon a-freeze, then the windy blackout, the deserted midnight,
The moon in a hollow tooth – such, once, were houses –

(Oh heart like a scarlet opal, who shall tell you as befits you?
Men and statues have fallen, a year has passed – but *they* did not
pass.)

The Exodus from Catalonia – Republican Spain walks into
France – Jan-Feb 1939

For these
France was a virgin field, a page open, ready
To write G r a t i t u d e on, a field for the ploughing-under of
pain,

A piece of calm after agony; they came as a gift here;
And so the flocks came, besides the gold and the cars and the
chariots defeated in hell –

But mostly came the hearts of men.

What was this frontier, tell me?

A pass for flocks,
A transient mile between those final rocks,
A strangulation with a shining end,
Hell's funnel –
     So they saw it, waiting 10,000 deep each day to climb their
                            gehenna.
Somewhere, sometime, between bristled sabres and stamping
                            platoons,
Peace! After the chesty sergeants and General Staff's barking
                      orders across their way,
Rest!
     And the Sister Republic answered:
       '*We hate you*'.

If these frontier things must be, they thought, next hours must
                        bring
That change when man becomes man again with his lamb at his
                        side,
On the green of earth resting, under an almost Spanish sun.
Climbing gehenna they thought:
Aren't we *seres humanos* – beings, human?
But the frontier – what is a frontier?
'Give us arms to fight or let us in' said the old man trudging
                    down back to Spain,
Telling me: 'Back to Junquera! Turned back!!
What means a 'frontier'? This! Now we search the ground
For any piece of food that might have dropped when we passed
                    before –
Back to Junquera for 'permits' – to enter what? France!
That is what this frontier means: *a line at the end of starvation*,
30 and more months of death, treacheries... all that has been...
72 am I. I was mayor of my place
In Asturias, and many a foul deed have I known,
But this, such as this, never! It is inconceivable.
All night we stood on that line, the 'frontier', in the roar of the rain;
I saw a woman give birth on the road, an old man die,

– Something like 3,000 of us there – people fainting, gangrene
                                        growing in wounds…
And now they turn us back. We are looking for food at our feet.
Have you seen anything one could eat? What should we do – ay,
                                        what shall we do?

I have seen I have seen
All this poor woof and weave, this drapery of exodus
Rotted with rain in one night here, transposed into compost,
A fit bed for the conqueror – along with one pale dead ass,
Les quatre fers en l'air, death's humble and monstrous belly;
Seen many a foul deed done, heard the hearts of men break,
Seen the blood of Spain's truth run dark – but no waste scrap of food.

'It is not right, compañero – they are mad in France, compañero,
Because it's coming to them the same tide;
We should have fought it till victory, we by their side –
But now, back to Junquera, with no crumb of food…'

Is there pardon for France and Franco in this in a mile of centuries?
The triumph of hell nears completion. A whole people has walked
                                        away.

The Lands That Were Today

To Kay Boyle

Ah listen, mark – the Devil's sick again.
It is night; it is Radio; it is the Danzig brew;
Noise of rushing rabble, shingle by arrogant sea,
Hush, hush, the demagogue's rampant.

How interesting, hideous but interesting, the noise of it all,
The key-drop, the holy tear in the voice between hiccups to Mars,
The down-slide, the mad uprush.. 'Humanität'.. the orchestration.
it's lasted…'Begeisterung am Menschen'…already one hour –

    Here in Normandy
    The stooks are set, the men gone in their millions to the East.

'Sie wissen hier genau' – oh voice of Devil-never-Fausted-with-
                       doubt –
We do, *genau* we do – the land that was Heine and Goethe.
Do not cut off the man's voice, pray, with your sticks to the fire,
Plague on your cooking-clatter; *listen*: a dictator bursts.

I am thinking: 'After the countries, he killed himself; yes, he
                       could try that,
But that is not enough; nothing can be enough.'

    … The land that was… Today 'finalism' without meaning.

On the wings of wine I am thinking, thinking, thinking,
Past-present-future, of something that will not go into words.
Tears have told it, tears buried with blood in revenge pendent in
                       Italy,
Something…how does it go…something like a quotation:
'How long, how long,
Dictator's stamping-ground the people's breast?'

What do we know of war? We know there is some kind of war,
Cynical, covert, cold, censored, a wraith-war, leashed holocausts,
There in men's East – but here, later, with lilacs, acacias,
Plaited round batteries, snapped – bleeding spring over corpses,
                                        over one I knew?
My village, my lovely land, my bit of eternal France…

Listen, tune in again, for the set is ending:
'Three years, says Britain. I, Hitler, answer, seven!
Siegheil!' (Oh their raucous hall and their gruff teutonic band)
And that is that,
                    and…

And then the Gallic cock lifted his spur
And the old lion woke out of his cynic rheums
And shook his claws, brushed fur and came alive again.
And all the tense driven pageantry of Empire got under way,
And we are forty now that knew the day
They killed Edward, Patrick, Raymond, Ivo, and my lover
In such fields' corners that are less England ever than is a stoop
                                        of mull by September stove –
Ay, it begins again, but it is different, for there are wars, and
                                            more, between;
And I have seen, I have seen,
Lived part of one, and shall again, I know;
And been
Where truth haunts rock and stone immortally round a people
                                        strong in the thigh;
I have seen them fight, and the fear of their truth used as order
                                        that they should die.

And now, dead men of England, lend me your ears
By the autumn stove, and from your timeless close,
Your chartless regions and unknowable spheres,
Communicate, pass by, or whisper what no man knows:
Is Humanity inching along? Is it 'Now', is it 'Not in our time'?
We are at one on it all – we are at one I suppose…

Journey to the New World

You, *mijito*, my son, my lover, my son,
You are free now, *free*…you that went to kill bulls in Avila
And found the priests with their guns there, the black snake with
                                                        its head up.
You are free – free to grieve still, but free to *live* again too.
We have left Europe, changed the North Star for the Southern
                                                        Cross.
Look! Here it all begins. It begins at Mendoza,
After the weary wonder of the Pampas in the Argentine's
                                                        dustrobe –
We drank beer without cease crossing them, thought of nothing as
                                                far as that's possible…
Look! Here it begins. We are in it. It has begun.

What does it mean, this note scribbled in the crazy car
Curvetting through a grey dawn, these words: 'The two passes –
                                                        Exodus?'
I remember – the Pass of death, the Pyrenean; the Pass to life,
                                                        the Andes;
The Andes, the Andes, the Andes – that is a name for life.
And then:
'Desprecio a la palabra en Europa, a la possia, a la verdad'.
You are eloquent my notes of that morning, you say further
(Of the sea-journey and arrival) 'It begins and it ends in colours,
Colour of sea in a hostile land, the white on the gray.'
Seven days anchored, waiting the convoy in the mouth of the
                                                        Gironde,
Frozen, benighted, spectral, raging, inarticulate –
Two hours at noon – for a painter, the white on the gray;
But for a poet, these: crispation, paralysis.
Ay, the end of France was the itch and the histoires de géndarmes,
A meet end, with its passes and permits, to a life there of twenty
                                                        years.
Start of the passage to the New World, the note says:
'Exit, suspended in pallor, pastels, Impressionists.'

We had Life-Belt and Life-Boat drill one day, the crew with gas-
                                                                masks,
A paternal captain and 172 scared Portuguese emigrants;
We had Lisbon at coaling-time, the black devils enacting hell
With their spades and buckets, and the roar of the coal down the
                                                                shute;
Cents a day for this, 20. We had Casablanca, Dakar,
Arab misery, giant Senegal, with Goree, past womb of pain;
Here the slaves came in their coffles, from here was 'the Middle
                                                                Passage' –
Today the old fort, the Slave-House, at last it is empty.
Dakar, foul with colonial purport, resplendent with Negro strength.
Days and more days – then the Equator,
A lake of milk and mirages and birds that were flying fish.
We had Rio – oh New World, you first at Rio...
Went ashore in a blast of Carnival, devoured you, adored you;
And Santos – oh harbours and tropics in a beauty that never ends.
And in Montevideo, friends, and the colours of Spain-my-Spain;
Another colour: waters of the Rio Plata before Buenos Aires;
It is the opal again, but a tawny and turbid opal, not that of Madrid.

The car – it is in the Andes now, and the note staggers:
'It ends with this, the Grand Approach,
It ends in Chile, with freedom.
Look! Here is the miracle,
And light on the miracle;
The light, you can almost touch it.
A cactus grows in the snow here, when it is the time of snows.
Look! These are cacti in the deep of the bend...
Look! Here are horses and no man near them,
For the horses here, they are wild, they are wild, they are free.
And then the great line of the summits, look, at the top of the curve,
Older than all the gods of earth, surging up at one go,
One higher than all the rest – all saying 'Eternity'.
Can we please leave our pain at the foot here, of the eternal snows
Where the highest says "Behold me: I am Aconcagua"?'

How many miles have we come? Here are no miles, only time,
Only continuance and colour mating with colour.
And then a note says:
'Gluck in a field composed, sometimes,
In a green field, on his piano, with golden wine
And birdsong and wind over flowers, and made such rhymes
And waves of sound all hearers wept with ecstasy…'
Why do I think of Gluck here – it is because of that, the ecstasy.
The Andes are singing to me; they are sound made visible, there
                              are words even in a message,
They pull me, they hold me, they say: 'Stay, you are part of us'.
And where are we now? In Uspalláta, the sole man-made in all of
                                                              this,
A tawny road reeling, an inn with waters and the *sauce lloròn*.
It is almost noon, and the car bounds on again –
And then and then, tell me my note, what did you say?
'I have *seen* noon here, noon burst open in all its colours,
Colour, eternal as stone by the Tomb of the Inca –
The colours change every few miles…
There is water here too, the Rio Mendoza.'
There is water…Here raged the waters of avalanche, the *aluvión*.
Destruction monumental on a scale with the Andes,
A few years back. And the driver said: 'Here too
Passed the armies of Liberation, General San Martin, and the
                              emancipation of the two countries
From the tyrant Spain.'
And my last note says:
'What is the frontier, tell me?
The Pass to Eternity –'

The journey is near its end – height carved out in rock, ridge
                                                        upon ridge,
A little train in a world of stone, descent into a green world, trees,
                                                        maize and water;
You are in Chile, *mijito*, you have reached the Promised Land –
All life is a long or a little train,
And weary the heart, the footloose heart, the Spanish heart

In its cell, beating and waiting, beating and waiting.
Take freedom today oh heart – for as to me
These things I saw them through a veil of pain…

Of pain, of pain – Ah how it comes
Repeating with a pulse of drums,
And seldom does their rhythm still –
Drums for the knife that's mate to love;
Love is my fate, love is my ill,
My inmost meaning, utmost loss,
My spring, my lock and key, my wild
Ninth wave that rages round your stone –
These things are nothing to you, child,
Maker of pain, undone by pain,
Or are they?
And must the tide and temper of it surge ever so?
Torero, what is your answer?
Or will these eternities we cross give me one?
This is what happens at the meeting of two elements –
There is pain and ferocity, and a measure of love.

What have the drums to do here in Eternity?
Intrusion of Europe's heartache, pain has come with us
And travels this road too in his swathe of grief,
And faces Aconcagua…

Thus we entered the land of the Condor.

The Chilean Sonnets

1
Chillán

Innumerable Pompeiis of the world,
This is your limbo, past and yet to be –
Between these wraths and rains and bumping sea
Man's hates and furies thrive – with courtesy
Out of forgotten Spain. But what is furled
Here in the rock is rock's, not for you, man.
Was it worth while, Conquistador? Chillán
Answers: Behold. The latent vagary
Of quakes commands – come flood, come June – at call,
Omnipotent, and triumphs the *roto*'s will
In drunken heart's ease... Ah this Chilián still,
This vat of drink to the lees... Then in it all
One poet issuing from that January tomb,
Experience gotten there for future's bomb.

2
Amaranth of Sunset

Done, undone, not done, and done too well –
Oh Chile of my despair, oh orb of thieves,
Oh whirlpool madness – oh you curious hell
Of love and hate, you cradle of all that grieves.
All Shakespeare vested in one small drunk man,
All of the poets in this love of mine,
All of the sorrows on that raft of wine;
Was this the man for me, the final man,
Who knows? Gone – to the amaranthyn last
Shaft as he watched it muttering 'Never more...'
I see my poet walking by the shore
Of time alone as I, locked in our past,
Snarling, quiescent. And then up speaks the wine:
'You to your life, *mijito*; I, to mine.'

3
At Dawn

No! I will sit and let the iambics play,
And I will wring the sonnet's neck and say
'Hell and eternity have met today
Here – and I, I defy them – come what may,
A stranger in your land, not more, at bay.'
And who has ears may listen if so he list,
Nothing will gain, oh nothing; ('amethyst
That keepeth away the fumes of wine', they say).
I will not talk or answer. All of my sphere
Lingers or centres on love that's gone, or here,
How can I tell, here in this transient room?
All is a lie, up to the uttermost tomb.
Nor would I know if all is done and lost –
Dawn is for ice, not for computing cost.

Psalm for Trinidad

I am Trinidad – Columbus discovered me,
Land of the Carib then, land of the palm trees, humming birds,
I am Africa, India now; gone are slaves and indentured labour,
The sons of these am I, the wage-serfs, under a still-Victorian
Union Jack.

(*Oh de sun de sun ha laash me; it 96 in de shade.*)

I am Oil and the reek and muck of it, the wage lost in the strike,
The worker's rotten barrack, the crusted, festering yard
Where life's not life but simply a six-score hard
Under a tin roof, five or six to a room; life is a sentence here.
80 cents, 60 cents, 50 or 35's my daily pay…
Slums of Empire – have you seen me, Lloyd George, to be calling
me that?

(What to do wid dis sun? When it not sun in come rain.)

I am Butler, Uriah Tubal Buzz Butler of the Oilfields,
A brown Negro man who wanted to make it a better life,
Started organising, spoke out, was jailed for it – with the Governor
                                                    saying: he is right,
And the Oil Co.s working the police, and the Governor sent away.

(Oh Gawd, oh Gawd, what he do, Butler? Butler must come again.)

I am the cane-break, the largest sugar-factory in the Empire,
Thin silent folk of India in those fields, dividends, engineers,
Bullock-carts, piety – brown hands splitting the golden cocoa-pods,
African faces in green depths, silent too, wondering 'how long dis
                                                    way?'

(40 cents, 20 cents – depend if I man or woman – it so, my day.)

I am Government House on its official lawn
Facing the Savannah – mine is no easy dawn.
I am Censorship suppressing, controlling, because here there is
                                                    always fear...
I am the white creole, the planter, paramount among the snobs,
I say it's a happy island, my summum bonum is the cocktail hour.
I am the Police Force and helmeted Colonialism rampant and
                                                    dominant.

(Here it get thirty days me for pick one fruit by roadside.)

I am Calypso, brown bards of the people improvising irony in song;
I am the multitude, the articulate, keen
Brown face and black and gold; the courteous Chinese
Trading in the towns, Indians passing mute almost ghostly;
I am the young hotheads, the cackle of old dark laughter, the ripe
                                                    vernacular on the roads...

(What about after de war, man you think it come the Democracy?)

I am Duprés, O'Connor, Gomes, Percival and Payne,
I am 'The People', the battling mayor of Port of Spain,
I am Kay and 'New Dawn', you can read the truth of me in this;
I am Gittens and Comma, brains that hold the import and savour
                                                          of me.

   (*Now dese friends for true, in deir writings, deir oratory.*)

I am Rienzi, walking between diplomacies,
Politics, politics – the burden sits heavy on me.
I am the poet Cruickshank, my Wordsworthian line
Sweeps oer the world and sculpts it, and I have done my time
In Colour's gusty battles. I am the anonymous force
Of human will, of hope for juster days soon.

   (*After de war, like for England for Trinity.*)

I am the Iron Music, the fork on the bottle with the spoon,
The drum out of Africa, the tambu-bambu, the collective Carnival;
Always always a note of sadness under the singing,
Always a wistfulness, an uncertainty, a back-bringing...

   (*Dis Carnival here, it our onliest own time in de year.*)

I am this voice in the night – (heard heard in the street):
'Dey call it New Year's Eve – Man, what new year is dis for we?
Workin' man can't eat, can't sleep, can't live properly;
Dis place it have nothin'; dis night it nothin' new for you or me..'

   (*New Year, Old Year, all de same for such as we.*)

   Trinidad, effervescent ---------
        look at me, look at me, look at me here.

'How Long?' Is Not 'For Ever'

Come look at us, islands that the Carib tide
Bathes with eternal swell; us, cocoa, palms,
Sugar and pitch and rum and oil – and psalms
Learned under slavery, pulsing yet inside
Men's toilsome breast and woman's. Come eventide
Their angelus outdoes the facts of day;
My dears, you are too good – 'please-God' – you pray
For that which is *your due*, and facts outride
All God-ward hopes. Yet 'God is our onliest friend'
You say to me. I know this too shall end
When the world's comrades muster to your side;
The planet's workers and the poet's pen,
Take them for allies – Truth is a rising tide –
My Africans, an answer comes to 'W h e n ?'

Less Than the Slave

She stood breast-high...yes, that is it, breast-high,
Faith with a cutlass armed in the still wood,
Amid the alien...yes, transplanted; stood
Saying 'If God spare life this ends, and I
Need work no more for twenty cents a day!'
Lily! You knot from Africa! You thing
Less than the slave of old – fill baskets, bring
Cocoa and coffee; pick those beans; *they'll* weigh.
So – you are worth two dimes, and men worth four
In those Antillian glades. Black, ragged, bowed
With agues, tired, illiterate – see their crowd
Dancing the cocoa on the drying-floor,
Democracies? Not here! IS as HAS BEEN –
Rulers, behold the sweet in your machine.

In answer to Trinidad's poet who asks me
'...What was it moved you to enlist
In our sad cause your all of heart and soul?'

To Alfred Cruickshank

My friend, ship rocks, and seas come great and small
Over the gunwale, but the captain reads
On, despite this. On land the teeming seeds
Breed without fear, and after the gusty fall
Of rain comes ready are they, present, erect,
Grown. Do you sense the symbol in it all?
The man outlives the storm, the tribunal
Of nature judges, tempering the elect.
Our lives are wars – You ask: 'Why love the slave,
The 'noble savage' in the planter's grave,
And us, descendants in a hostile clime?'
Call of the conscious sphere, I, nature and man,
Answer you: 'Brother, instinct, knowledge... and then
Maybe I was an African one time.'

14 Juillet 1941

In the trough of the wave, in the pit, the very nadir
Of all – what's in your sack, Time, for the likes of we:
Fortitude, perseverance, defeats, suspense most horrible, then
                                more endurance?
Best that we cannot tell – or would I rather see

The heart of the blackness bared, the ultimate, present whole
At its closest, the total corruption in the skull?
More and more communal is man's grief – yet each tragedy is
                                solitary –
Europe, you sea of pain – how long is this tide at its full?

Fragment in the Old World

Here comes an angry little moon,
A russet bauble in an indifferent sky –
Who wrote 'It may be Prester John's balloon',
And who 'Theirs not to think but do and die?'
Oh fitful quotes, your strophes ring like the hours,
Be gone, and let me get my furrow straight –
Oh quotes that want to glove each circumstance
And lead the poet to your Walpurgis dance,
Be gone.

Gin we drink from weariness,
Gin we drink through dreariness,
Metal-mouth gin, desist – serve us no quotes today.

'Theirs not to think...'
In Lybia, Penang, or the old imperial sequence –
But theirs to think and do in Russian snows...

Incarnations

This was the kind of man with his hands on the tiller
Of the little old ship riding wave like a cockle or rocket,
Landing in deep surfs, beaching her sharply, then striding forward
Questing or conqueror over the frozen turf of the north.
He stood on the tops of hills and arid summits
In most extraordinary dawns that started the tremendously long
day with a ritual –
Days longer in ventures than sunlight –
And he would always be planning and thinking
'What is the *best* we can do with these new ones,
For them as well as us... amalgamate this handful of people...'
He was a kind conqueror,

Knowing strength and sanity and the balance of heart, mind and
                                                              hand.
Finally the day would come to an end. Then he would lie down
In the sheepskins and bearskins and the imported arctic feathers
Of breasted duck and teal, the gold head easy in all this brown
                                                          and rose
For a little, with a primitive lute-string
Somewhere near, being played for sleep by a heap of hot embers;
All of this very warm in the improvised huts of conquest and in
                                              the home castles.
The shadows were huge then, and the drink strong, very strong;
Was it athelbrose or ale or mead or the berry from the woods...
Whatever, it was made rich and strong, for the transports of
                                              strong tired men.
And in the splendour of blazing logs
Winked a power of great stones, precious ones, with the
                              far-travelled amber amongst them.
The man sat, thinking and planning still, at the head of the table,
                                                          silent,
While the new things were brought in from the outlying provinces,
And a message about gold, with news of further tradings,
And pondered while the rest toasted conquest: 'What is the *best*
                                          way t use all this?'
And then, after a few centuries,
He is one of two in the interview of two kings –
Look, the same head, eyes that appraise, analysing,
The same build, the same muscling, the poise;
A leader, a poet, one for the arts, but also for statecraft,
One that honours line and the shapes and meanings of flesh –
A meeting of two kings that is going to end the bloody battles;
One of the two is defeated but I do not know which.
It seems as if this man is persuading the other
That even the conqueror does not win;
Life will not halt or dwell on these concepts: *acceptance* of defeat,
                                          triumph of victory.

Such a condition is useless, it does not work.

It does not work for the victor to sit on the vanquished
With armies and tyrannies, rough law-codes, impositions:
'These are the dragon's teeth'.

And another time,
Trekking across an American desert, with a flask and a banjo
                                                    under the arm,
Pioneer, buccaneer, emigrant, prospector –
Learning the solitary crag, affiliate with the empty plain;
Night in the juke-box – man's brother; gone by dawn,
On, west. And then a long poem written about the time of sundown
Under a wind-carved pillar, with a vague-à-l'âme – but also with
                                                    a plan.

(Down that long slant of centuries the metal is always gold,
Old Celtic gold, and the thread blue, that blue and green and grey
Of certain flints – and eyes – that blue as much stone as sea,
Pristine, eternal.)

Force out of old northern time: 'Contigo pan y cebolla',
The Spanish says it best: 'Sufficient with you bread and onion';
More is not asked, all being here – forgetting never:
War within war, man within life, life within struggle –
These must be won.

Whose Desert?

Bou Ahmet Ben Sikri Bey foresaw a war;
It came: two hundred thousand into Spain.
Jusef evoked the Riff, baring a scar,
And cursed the *roumis*; then came war again.
Hussein on a car was in it, and at times
Too crazed to pray, then called to Allah: 'Heed!
Blow then a stench *accidiae* from your climes

And raise your devils from the Shott Jerid.'
And Maître Tahar, his Tunis now the world,
Mused in a masterly Arabic: 'Carthage stood
Where guns now shake and deathly smokes are curled,
Fasces and Swastika – death to their brood –
But after annihilation of these dogs
Whose conquering wing above our Islamic rags?'

Dordogne

Creysse, Lot, on bank of Dordogne,
Two hundred souls, their oxen, truffle-pigs,
A grey village round a blond castle-keep,
Puffed out with trees, the night-sky prickled with stars
O-brightest-of-all in September-crispest-of-all;
The talk earth-flavoured, the smell of the hot cep in it all
Through the wine and garlic –

Do you remember, Henry
We were there that 1930, and I made you work;
After the day's bucket brought in from pump
You sat at the piano the oxen had dragged from Martel,
Composed *Henry-Music* and were loved by the people of Creysse:
'A brown man, a beautiful Negro, in a red and blue car…dropped
                                              from the sky…
Now look how he plays' they said, and we all drank together at
                                              the inn.
We didn't look so much at the world then, that pre-Marchukuo
                                              year,
The village was the scene, not death's international roustabouts.
One night I sat on our grey steps and saw her, the old crepuscular,
Bowed over the boiling, the whole boiling, and wrote of her – this:

Steams, but not in any now-dry now-flooding river washes

All the sheet and weave of the region in a slow stew;
Her copper's a day of judgement, compost of noon and night
                                                            stuff,
Filed-sweat, tavern-sweat, love-sweat, death-sweat, all of it,
Heats of maize and tobacco acre, roads and the boisterous
                                                          market.
Lifting – oh lay brotheress – all these robes smartly, while she
                                                          grieves
To a little girl attendant of the grease that groans
In crease's prison, of the tears
Old dribble and spent sweat print on the square of
Shirts, of the tortured *strings*, telescoped, corkscrewed
Enfeeblement of *pot-wipers*, wrenched *bib, kerchief* invalidate
Its colour-with-age-I-tell-you prismed,
And the plain dust itself in the *apron*!
Shameless this tough green
Woollen that will no down, with its goose-gabble.
Hierarchy – the big ones go underneath,
The ill-though-of *valence* and the history of a windy night –
Cheek by jowl by *towel sheet*,
Et la *serviette éponge* qui sut se marier;
Mayor's *frill* drover's *wipe*...
That *summer-blouse* was before her first –

The graillon's in the glory-hole...soot!
Blood's brown braggadocio come to your reckoning...
Auspice! Hog spit on it – vanishing of vanities –
Cunning the red winestain: to ink thou shalt return.

Not a bubble out of the load,
Appointed all, with a quiver of *socks* at copper-brim,
And here's a month's chat slowly, slow-ly...
Old yes-and-no woman
DOWN with the stars into the pot
And UP with the devil – company's company
...Where a pin's none... Sangdieu!

She sets four stones
Cardwise on her stacked pyramid, and the sparks prick
Fire into charcoal nightlong, and she pats it...
'Si c'est pas *honte* de ne pas envoyer tout ça plut tôt –
A perishin' shame on them sending me all that at one go.'

Dordogne,
Land of the walnut, chestnut, goose and vine,
(Land of red hearts), land of caves prehistoric.
Chellan, Magdelanian, Musterian, Cro-Magnon man
Left more than a line or two here: the rump of a bison
Limned in ochre or umber, the curve of a feline
Crouched, the span of a taut bow.
Land of red hearts – today the *masquisards* are on the *causse*
In the sparse thyme of winter, raking of the shepherd's hut
A stockade with bombs and rifles, somewhere there above
                                                    Rocamadour
Somewhere above Marennac, and Fages, the great ruin,
Places like that –
The red heart turned into armed fists against the Boches and Vichy
On the causses, the high stony remote empty hilltops –
Salut, best of peoples and regions; we shall meet again.

Dordogne,
All day in Lascave's entrail the stalagtite drips to the stalagmite.
Dorgdogne,
All day all day wives wash against your stones...

O time with dual face, now whole, now facet,
Speed the great battles. *Mort à l'envahisseur,*
And to all traitors, double death.

Previously Unpublished
or Uncollected Poems

Soldiers Fallen in Battle

These die obscure and leave no heritage,
For them no lamps are lit, no prayers said,
And all men soon forget that they are dead,
And their dumb names unwrit on memory's page.
Pale heroes when their ghosts are all assembled
On the dry, untilled fields of common death,
No man to number them with living breath,
And nothing there that to this life resembled.
Their ways were set to meet the paths of war,
There opened a low sea of deadly strife,
And they sank deep, surrendering this earth's life,
And were made prisoner and enchained therefore,
But none cared deeply in the morning crowd,
Who walked like hypocrites, with bare heads bowed.

Remorse

I have been wasteful, wanton, foolish, bold,
And loved with grasping hands and lustful eyes
All through the hectic days and summer skies,
And through the endless streets; but now am old
And ill and bad – content with discontent,–
Enduring the discomfort and the blows
With sunken head and heart that shaking goes.
Resigned to sit and wait in punishment,
A martyr without claim, a parody
Of classic crowned apostles and sweet saints
Now praised in marble and in gorgeous paints
Or singing in loud scores of harmony....
I sit ashamed and silent in this room
While the wet streets go gathering in their gloom.

Uneasiness

Tonight I hear a thousand evil things
Between the panels and the mouldering floor;–
Small bitter things with hearts and, maybe, wings,
That curse their bondage yet entreat for more
Free wicked time and space to hurt our lives,
And bring unthought of ill-luck to us all;
Undreamèd horrors, stories of old-wives,
Armies of corpses hid behind the wall
That creep and grind and tear each other's souls
And fight with devils in a horrid tongue,
Making sleep flee away beyond the Poles....
All this I know, although the night is young
And ling'ring breathless, full of timid fear,
Waiting in terror for *their* hour that's near.

Brigit

Here, at that time, sat a woman – I see her yet
In the full of all her colours, I see her close,
Her green eyes growing strange, certain green turns strange
When some particular mood runs into it,
Then goes full green again.
Her hair, how red, how red, nor fox; nor ruby,
Nature had made of it one of its mysteries,
An air-filled moss it was, and it also frothed,
Water and breeze together in harmony
Above the pale, most gothic, perfect face.
She moved as fine hands move along harp-strings,
In such dresses as might be supposed to enrobe such things:
One was sea-green, with veils that floated and swam,
One, a pale poppy-red, with green, of same kind,
One in that blue and red that have come together

To put the sunset's battle out of mind.
I think there was also a heavy purple dress
Sewn with ancient golden coins…What contradictions!
For, all in all, she was The Aquamarine.
                    Her name was B R I G I T –
Born only in such times was such a queen.

Victor and Nancy at Pertenhall
in Feb, Say, of the Early Fifties

Morning begins with a boot thrown by an irate colonel
Across the floor below, in a shower of pills,
With the cousin above, half-young, half-old, cursing on waking up
At the ghastly onomatopoeia (what is it called, aerophagitica?)
L'aérophagie – air-balls in plain English in the stomach,
                                oppressive, day-long, day-long,
Wind on the heart – in plainer English yet.

Then, after the painful ascension into day for both of us,
Comes the hour of the silver gin tray a few minutes before lunch,
And a gulped double is taken by the colonel, now restoring
                                himself –
(Who never was anything of the kind, but was just Cousin Victor);
The cousin of above (me) drinks slower, savouring it all.
And then comes nice, quick English lunch in the Adams dining
                                room,
With our ancestor portraits, how well hung, on the walls there:
Cunard, Cunard, Cunard, and Cunard again – I say to myself
Realising suddenly that the colonel *has finished* before I've even
                                put fork to plate…
Oh dear, oh dear, this tardiness of mine – perhaps due to the
                                aerophagitica?
But *why* will he ask me what *I* think of world affairs
At the moment itself I try to push deep freeze peas into my mouth?

Then comes a long, beautiful drive across invisible Midlands
Cousin Victor driving so well, less walrussy now, it seems,
And my aerophagitica gone (alas how temporarily) –
And so – let's say – we are going to splendid old Hinchinbrooke
                                                    Castle,
Across the ever-flat of Beds and Hunts,
With its delicate colouring that only some dead French painter
Would know how to set down, or want to – I'd be thinking,
Cousin Victor driving on, smooth as silk, exploding at 'these
                                      preposterous females'
On their rocking bicycles 'with their great, beastly breasts!'
'How true,' I think, 'that pair of she-hogs, pah! And their hellish
                                      colours so close together:
Pink and canary yellow – an apricot mixture of woollies –
Pumping along with their great sagging breasts,
In the way of the colonel, too, on this smooth MacAdam road,
Of the invisible, misty Midlands.'

And so we nearly arrive at lovely Hinchinbrooke Castle
(Cromwell's relics are there, its hostess an old friend),
When up comes a column of local Borstal boys,
Marching, by order, in enforced file,
And I, who want to smile or even shout at them 'Good-day, good-
                                                    day',
Guessing what prison life must be – out of sheer sympathy –
Am silenced by the colonel shooting a sharp look at me, from
                                      one round icy, blue eye...
And then we say to each other, simultaneously:
'What shall I leave you, darling, when I die?'

And so we arrive at Hinchinbrooke, all my aerophagitica, thank
                                                    god, gone.

And then we sit and talk by the glorious open fire,
With darling Rosemary, hostess, mother of six, how young yet
                                      and fine, and very handsome,
And I think: *'Your dad was certainly un grand sabreur,*

That is, he was ever and ever after all and any a skirt,
Any skirt seemed to attract him, your dad, that grand
         "bottoms-up" man, Ralph Peto;
And you, dear welcoming Rosemary, are his daughter,
Out of lovely on-drinking Ruby, the Scot – that I knew when
        both of them were first engaged...
Oh yes, how time passes...'

Grown children come in now to the blaze and glow of the logs,
Drinks are had, old books, so finely kept, looked at and admired,
And then the colonel stands up, in his twenty-pounds worth of
        splendid English shoes,
And back we go motoring in the dark the thirty miles or so to
          Pertenhall;
And then again the lovely drink tray, after our boiling baths,
And the good, gulped-down dinner, with the ancestors looking on,
And then back again to the wonderfully warm sitting room, with
        its pink and blue chintzes,
Its ineffable taffetas curtains, blue-green turquoise painted walls,
        and panelled door.
Twenty could well sit here, but thank god, only the two of us – I
        think – for the moment, together,
With our talk about all the hithers and yon of a possible next
        world war,
And the colonel getting cross, and, I suppose, perplexed at me;
'No, no! Well, yes, another tiny drink – indeed, why not?'
And then Victor, no longer the walrussed colonel, turns on the Radio,
And what comes out of that? Goons, admirable Ustinov, and
        Bach in excelsis...
Then again our preposterous talk about next war, and more,
With Victor saying 'You're too subjective and emotional, and all
        that,
But...well...that's why I love you, after all.'
I saying: 'Not at all, not at all. Despite my dreadful aerophagitica
I *am* writing my book, here, now and every day
On George Moore, and come of it what may. Yes, darling, despite
        all our asperities,

I thank you, coz, for your company, the darling dogs, and the
                                                              facilities
Of here and now – and how, and how, and how!'
(Oh Lor', oh Lor'
I could take my head into my hands, remembering those times,
                                                    even now...
Gone, gone for ever – and Tony died there before,
As I saw, and lengthily saw.)

Then finally, but not so late to bed;
As we go up those cold and lovely stairs,
The Silver Fox gleams down (that was father's in 1881),
That you, Victor, housed for me after its nigh-thirty years sepulture
                                            in my London bank;
And then I think already: 'Tomorrow's another day,
When Cousin will be transmuted into Colonel Walrus once more,
And 'All's to do again', as Shakespeare knew.'

What's done is done and finished, done for ever.
And damn this pother and fuss about 'future wars';
All life's a bundle of broken shards and spars,
With a few touches of yellow, red, green, blue
To prick the heart a little further, further,
But that's no thing of patience, ever, ever;
There *is* no consolation, never, never,
Take it or leave it, all's one, in this century's weather...
Yes, I suppose they'll come, those future wars,
Indeed I do – bearing yet greater sores...
But now to bed and sleep – even if one wakes up
Smack at 3.30 AM, though why? The cup
Of mind-thought-heart has overbrimmed, maybe,
Even in sleep – Oh lord, dear me, po' me;
Am I so overbrimmed with 'ought' and 'naught',
Lying, quiescent, in this lovely bed,
Possessed day-long by my single George Moore thought,
All pencil spent,
In lieu of tea with Victor down below?
What one likes best, one clings to most – For me?
Just pad and pen.

And so in bed, solus, worn, always sad,
Suddenly waked by the thought 'What's good, what's bad?
Oh me, po' me – better to be just dead?'
And then the pricks of 'Yet again tomorrow,
That morning start with the boot, oe'r harrow and furrow
           Of yesterdays and yester-years, with ills
All incommensurable for all the pills...
Po' you, po' me...'

                Pipe down, and try to sleep;
Naught can be done, *forever,* against tomorrow.

Pain Sonnets

1

I think I know what they sang in those old halls:
One man, maybe, had a stringent stance on PAIN,
Caused by no viper's lance, but by arrow-rain
Down-hurtling on man and horse and fields and walls
In the fire hither-and-you of battle's rage.
Leaving out fear, his theme may have been sheer PAIN,
What it will do to a leg, and, ay, to a brain,
In its strange upsurge and decrease on the self-same page
Of *one*, day, perhaps. Till, like a setting sun
Enveloping all in its purple agony,
Came PAIN again – now in black ecstasy –
To lord and vassal, both, and both were done.
I think that one, maybe, mayhave thought of such:
A lone, tired man. Of his kind there were not much.

2

Be a thing said for once and all, then never again:
Be it said sharp, sheer, and neat, then never again,
And alone, on one single string of a violin
Before the full chords of pain come mounting in,
In their majestic surge, their inexplicable wonder,
Their strange plush-colours, their algebra, their thunder
Around the wound, up-rising from bone to brain,
Their mathematics and their calculations,
Their strangely Arab designs and Turkish fashions...
    Where goes all this, while the sow-slow passing days
    Hold down bad blood beneath their heavy finger?
        Stamp well on the ground then, man, both deep and well;
        Stamp fast, then slow, on pain, and then again,
            Man, if thou cans't!

3

Interminable length of winter afternoon!
Man flat of his back, cupped in a swathe of pain,
  Thinking of much or of nought. All's one in such hours,
A-drowse would be best, till that vision of arrow-rain
  Shocked him awake, with its 'All's to be done again'.

      'How to fight on, when a good three-quarter lost
    Seems of my battle now, in this furious game
    Of life? Let me think! No, think I cannot today...
    Yet that last quarter, bound to be wind-tossed,
    Even it, in the rain-borne hours, shall I hold it, say,
To mould it as I would wish, till its brief while
    Expire at last on that vast, impressive pile,
    That growing mound of all the centuries?
        Not likely's that!'

Stripling

'None knows enough, for all speak in foreign tongues',
A new-come stripling then sang, 'and yet time runs
From its unknown bud to continuity'.
We saw those arrows fall on your walls today
As we approached. All was twixt hell and well,
For you, then them, then you. Indeed, amain,
The battle wheel turned fast. *It will turn again,*
We know for sure – When-where no one can tell.
          But there are finer things within my strings!
I am of tomorrow, today and yesterday.
What do you think it means when music rings
Its hammers upon the anvils of poetry?
My curse be on your roses *and* your slings,
The devilish pair, the flowers atop the words,
The unknowable roots, then the outburst of swords!
One thing called 'End' shall come to us all one day...
And death to all wars as well, for ever and aye."

To Professor Bernelot Moens

Race hatreds and prejudices are to be conquered by comprehension and appreciation of the character and intellect of the diverse peoples of the world. Only then will these injustices be wiped out. This is the theme of Professor Bernelot Moens, the famous anthropologist. The 'Dutch Darwin' classifies humanity throughout the ages as follows: Primitive man, civilised man, humanised man, cultured man, perfect man. He has created the concept of the Supra-Nation, beyond delimitation of nationality. This is the condition-to-be of perfect man – in the future. It is a plan of his that the 'Supra-Nation' shall cruise round the world. May it be a cruisade as well to abolish class prejudices and voice the demands of Science for a 'One world' terrestrial sphere, for the good of the entire population of the world.

Primitive, conscious, civilised, cultured – blood
Of the world in fusion to make perfect man;
Races are equal; this, the future's plan...
Between the proving skulls he'd passed, now stood
At gaze upon the nations' wars and rages.
Time weaves the white with yellow, brown and red
Despite the hatchets round the mating-bed,
The rank battalions of the Saxon sages.

The Supra-Nation crests the racial seas,
Docks in new sunset splendours, where the great
Banquet transcendent science that no State
May triumph over. Yet, my friend, what frees
The peon's hands that raised the warrior's shield,
The loin-clothed coolie in the paddy-field?

To Douglas Cooper from Nancy Cunard

Lines inspired by his 1964 New Year's Card

All that I ask of the years: no fuss, no fuss!
Nor will there ever be twixt you and me,
For both can ask, and get, from each of us,
The wherewithal of continuity.
Old Year, New Year, all's one and the same to me.

Dear man, this nineteen hundred and sixty-four,
What is it but a knock upon the door
Of part-surprise, part-probability?
Must we have fears, and can we plan at all...
You think we'll dribble to some 'dying fall'
The poet wrote of? No, nor you nor I
Will wanton, aimless, between sea and sky:
You, with you splendid gift of hither-and-yon,

Your *sabidurìa* (knowledge), and your taste –
You think such things do ever go to waste?
No, we shan't drip into some 'dying fall'.
You, you'll drive on, battling against the hosts
Of those who'd turn the artists into ghosts
With no esteem but irony; you'll talk,
Ever, I fancy, as easy as others walk,
Along some carefree lea.

I shall go on, I think, writing always
About the Spain of yore, wherein my days
Burst into life, a-listen, and so thus saw
What never again shall be no more, no more...
Thus in some strange, yet inexplored bud,
Tomorrow may rise into erect manhood...

Amid the dust and valour of what blood?

For Douglas Cooper

With the postcard of Eze-la-Vieille, La Haute, et même la Hautaine

A castle in all its ruins, behold, behold...
Cut out snake-lizard of the promontory,
See sea as sky, its importance will then stand up
Despite the wrack of century on century,
Importance and impotence well matched together...
Ah mon ami, mon frère, what to do with Time's weather?

Passport to Freedom

France

Some truths flame, incandesce – others like the blue
Deep of the timeless fiord, or fires seen through husk of ice,
Wait. Truth is hate. This is France. No other necessity's
Afoot in the corn, in the coal-mine, erect on the castle at Saverne
In the full of the banished Tricolor, the one put back there.

France is married to grief, bears grief's brood, is grief's cold widow;
The name of her peace is 'death'. This, after the breaking of the
                pulses
The heart staggered, the brain convulsed, the nerves paralysed.
Somewhere in it all remained the empty zero hour –
Hate enters the zero hour; good. This womb shall bear life again.
Who is hate? She has made him her only lover,
Single in purpose as a magic; as luminous, as multiple as star-dust.

Hate like a little familiar animal has the freedom of the house,
The freedom of road and city. There is hate in a *sou*,
Hate in a crumb, in the grinding of tram-wheels,
In the *vin du bistro*, and the mumbling monologue,
Hate in a harlot's shoe, in the priest's breviary leaves,
In the oil greasing a lathe, and the cobbler's broken awl.
Hate backwards and forwards, in the axles turning and all their
                echoes,
In the May Day *muguet* and the iron flowers of November,
Hate in leaves fallen and in red buds to come,
in the breeze and the frost and the pool, in all the dying and
                renewing,
Hate climbing the curve of the circle –
Look, look, how the womb fills – like a moon approaching the full.

Italy

I

I wonder – is Benozzo still a-flower,
And does the spring still mount the Umbrian hill…
History, a plain, and Italy the tower
That dominates; this is high tide of ill.
Tyrants before; feuds; daggers turning grey
Conspiracies to scarlet; tyrants now;
The Roman worker on the Appian way
Bowed but resilient; hunger's broken plow
Driven across the land. *Their* Trasymene,
Your Abyssinia. Soldiers, peasants, men,
Stifled, with raging hearts, that wait the day
To hurl their satrap from the outraged scene.
They will not spare when answer rings to: '*When?*'
This blood comes first – then all their flowers of May.

II

Fiorelli… hilltops…blue of the hyacinth
Under Orvieto, and Cortona's spring;
The cow is led to her curvetting king;
Gone, winter's shrouds; and in the ruined plinth
Valerian reddens – Time bears on its bones,
River-deliverer – and the rain's spears
Are conquerors turned to lovers; April bears
While the gold stonecrop's busy in the stones.
In the year's firstness, *prima vera*. This
Perennial mystery I see not more
Doubtful than is your change – your change not less
Certain than is that fury on the shore,
That fact of waves tides' ultimates express,
Risen, like you, from *shall be*, to: *it is*.

III

Tomorrow is Matteotti, and all those dead.
Tomorrow: the dead Rossellis, and all the slain.

Tomorrow: my Giacomelli – you that were Spain
Too, fought you not for her? Ay, in one bed
Our wills for her together one moment lay,
With the black night's rifles for their mating song.
Tomorrow: Nitti, and the martyr's throng –
Ah dead and living, how you shall fill that day.
Dante, long gone. But Dante, eternal *you*,
Wrote: 'Italy's tomorrow, rich and free
And all-resounding', and the prophecy
Out of this keep of pain and wrath shines true.
Oh dual Janus of the conflicting hours,
Your swords lie in the ground beneath your flowers.

Russia – The U.S.S.R.

I see a man standing sharp against the skyline, a woman on the
                                                        horizon,
Born in a vast October, guarding the East and West of life.
It is here they say: 'No citadel we cannot take in the end.'
Was it Lenin? It *is* all. This is the U.S.S.R.;
The giant's come of age in the blood bath; The giant arms him
                                                        hurricanes
Of driving steel, and with little snowflakes
So close, so close – and so unending; arms him with emptiness,
Hunger and the burnt acreage of near-infinity,
With great leaders, partisans, galloping heroes,
With moujik wickedness, with Death's inexhaustible tricks –
Ah, Death's both Slav and Tartar.

The giant slept so long in the world, awakened in Russia;
You had forgotten his name – his old simple name which is: Truth.
He stirs,
And the false-measure half-tone vices fall way.
He moves,
And between YES and NO pass the armies of pristine values.
He stands,
And a forest of hands sweeps towards him; not a race lacking.

He arms,
He is Truth fully armed now – millennium is on its way.
Vnoushenie, inspiration – you giant that gives us our life again.

All of the agony is going to turn into something else
When the time is won to turn.
It is then we shall honour our dead and our martyrs
With revenge, and with tears eternal as amber; then will we
                                                drink to them
With laughter too, knowing they will be seeing us, having helped us,
Knowing they will want it so, ordering our laughter:
Laughter, comforting scarlet of strength, plenty, comradeship.

BUT TODAY
The only red's on the snow: bayonet red.
The next colour, they'll call it: Peace. Let us wish it: World's peace,

       MIR Y POBIEDA
       Peace and Victory

Spain

Now – remember the Heart.
Not much is known of it,
For so the heart is and was ever, not much known about.
Write…of little water drops making a river
And the river sub-terrene, the fuller for the damming.
Write…of revolt and revenge, and waiting,
Of planning and the sporadic *golpe de mano* on the mountain,
Truck-train of munitions for Germany blown up,
The anonymous dead, here and there, its import a very hinge
But the event furled into itself, the *cosecha* later
When whatever year it be orders the harvest.
Write of the Heart – they'll understand you, the Spaniards will.

This land
Is a palimpsest – is it not –

Scored over and over with pain,
And with strength furrowed, and hammered with endeavour.
An example
Of how waiting tempers the coming sword.
Here nothing is lost – no vagueness, no compromise
In the plain straight line of things
As they should be – and will be.

Numantium –
     That pain is gone, passed into time's earth
With Cervantes to fight it again. (Oh Father Ebro,
And a skull-full of Romans, and the Numantian fury.)
Done, it is over. A.D. 150. But the temper of it's left:
Resistance, Death: palimpsest. Spain is guerrilla
Into the hills gone, where no *guardia* can follow,
Nature and man – rock and Spain – as ever united here.
Not the crafty Nazi,
Nor the mechanised hysteria of machines
Reduces. And if the iron rain come again?
You cannot put out a volcano with dynamite.

You will want to look back on that war – see it as a ridge
Blocking capture – without arms much – very high,
And the city of Madrid, the heart, the *fortaleza*,
Wall of the world, rampart against the Fascist tide.
See it as hunger and the unheated room
With the Castilian wind through the winter shell-holes there,
The drawn, thin face, the gaunt, crazy meal,
Sandbags and cold – the bean in all its nakedness.

     Battle without weapon,
     Battle with starvation,
     Battle against treachery –
     Now, battle of waiting.

It is not necessary, as elsewhere it *is* necessary
To send the message along: 'The country will rise again';
They need no trumpets they whose being is the whole of this.

We're a long way from all of that here now...
And then, a pair of eyes burning in a pub one night:
Led the British in the I.Bs. then
                    Yes, time is a train,
Our train, and we know it, Sam, will conquer the longest track...
A long long way from the inspiration here now
This London '42's October, yet here is a brand,
You, travelling fire, *camarada*: I name you, Sam Wild.

Germany

Dedicated to John Heartfield

1

Öd und leer
Eine wüste –
Bavarian dreamer where are you today?
    'In Dachau, Buchenwald – *bin Moorsoldat*,
A soul on a moor where Death and Time are warders.
A soul? With a body forsooth; the body, a ball and chain
Dragged until out by order of the bullet
Or torture in the hideous dawn or the last vesperal flogging.
    Knife, lash and hatchet:
See the scutcheon of the *Herrenvolk*.
    Once this was a human land,
An old grey green river between castled vineyards and legends,
The dappled Rhineland and the smile between the apple trees,
And Heine's songs – here the heart wandered like a lover –
Aus meinem grossen Schmerzen
Mäch Ich die kleine Lieder;
I know not what we can make of ours,
The cofferdam's full to the brim but leaded with silence.
    This was a place once
Of spirit and intelligent courage;
Now they've turned life into *Ersatz*
In Hackenkreuzland – and where the hammer strikes
It strikes alone to break and not to make...'

And a voice rang over the moor
'*Todt ist kein Ersatzding im Russischen Schnee*'
(No, death's no ersatz in the Russian snows.)

'You remember öd und leer? It referred to a sea
Where no sail showed – it is Wagner's *Tristan* –
Came the sail bearing Isolt, and the tune changed
Late, late – too late, for all its joy. So for us, late
Is the sail over the waste of years, the flute plays to very many dead,
Falters, resumes. It will not bring back Erich Mühsam.'

Another said:
'While you chattered "peace in our time" and everything shook
                                        because the base was rotten,
Hugged child whispering 'Can't happen here', keeping your
                                        politics warm on the hob,
And the facts swelled in their ghastly sequence leering back at
                                        you in the chapter called Munich,
We were here with our pickaxes, spades,
In our fog, our fury, our silence;
Here were we – we, the veterans.'

                    2
A travelling wind blew over the dirty snow
With a clang of battle and a song in it, and a man said:
'That is our Thaelmann Kolonne in the streets of Madrid.'

In the sullen northern dusk the shadows come and go,
Look close, each is alive and most are strong;
And the mist turns into sound, the sound into singing:
    'Victory, though not the action –
    I have seen Victory coming but not the action,
    The way, the year it will come.'

When the tide bursts free remember this and these,
Saying: *Not conquest of men but victory over war*,
And what makes it, the Hackenkreuz, the Fasces.

England

Soldier, poor Soldier

Stands like an ox, man, 'as 'is beer at the bar,
Soldier poor soldier
Cum frum the Midlands, dumb as the Stoke wot bore 'im,
Soldier poor soldier
Tur git tur this...e wunders... whoi wur Oi born?
Soldier poor soldier
'E shuffles 'is feet an' now 'e's thinkin' o' missus.
Soldier poor soldier
Soon 'e'll be wroitin' 'er, tellin' 'er: 'Bear up, muthur,
Soldier poor soldier
Oi'm fur the draft, Oi'm shiftin' tur Overseas...'
Soldier poor soldier
'E's thinkin': 'She'll be that puff-eyed when she gets it.'
Soldier poor soldier
''Ere's whur tur wroite me' 'e'll put, 'and moind you keep that
Soldier poor soldier
Patch o' greens cumin', and also yur upper lip
Soldier poor soldier
'Ard. 'Ere's whu to wroite: 1,543,670,
Soldier poor soldier
WP/Base Camp – that's Overseas –
Soldier poor soldier
That's moi address no mistake; and don't you make
Soldier poor soldier
No silly mistakes with it, muthur, and then Oi won't
Soldier poor soldier
Make no mistakes withe War' – wud that make 'er laugh?
Soldier poor soldier
'You wus 40 last birthday, and 'ere am Oi 46:
Soldier poor soldier
Got thru the last, and Oi'll manage tur git through this
Soldier poor soldier
Some'ow, Oi expect, but muther it do seem 'ard;

Soldier poor soldier
And then it doan' seem so 'ard
Soldier poor soldier
And then it doan' seem so 'ard if everyone pullin'
Solider poor soldier
'Is weight tur make it the last, the bluddy last
Soldier poor soldier
O' all these wars – but is it? 'Ere's love and kisses;
Soldier poor soldier
The men's alroit – but Oi'm thinkin' o' you and 'ome.'
Soldier poor soldier
'E 'as 'is second and get to thinkin' o' England:
Soldier poor soldier
Not much of a Peace it wur between the two,
Soldier poor soldier
And not it's the 'Uns again, the Nazi nasties;
Soldier poor soldier
Jap's still cheeky, and Empire's going' down drain.
Soldier poor soldier
Expect Oi'm fur India, fur 'Allah's Paradise'
Soldier poor soldier
Like the picture 'ad it – Oi'm fur old paradise...
Soldier, poor man.

The Poet to His Wars

(For John Gawsworth)

The poet in a trench at sunset, awaiting battle. He goes on thinking, at times talking to his rum-flask, and all is imminent. 'As good a time as another, or what better, to set it down at last, the definition, to me, of inspiration, or do I mean of poetry? While waiting like this, what better?'

1

Of poetry? Sometimes it comes in a tear
That rises here, there, anywhere, alone;
Back to the heart it goes to suffer there.
At times it comes on wings of wine, then's gone
Back to nowhere, nowhere.

2

Twilit it comes, or in a burst of gold
Is all around – sunset in Mexican skies –
You may be sure it's nature's not yet told,
All's in hiatus between doubt and lies;
A poem? Not to be sold!

3

A poem is like a wind held fast in a tree
That shakes because the wind's got into the bush,
Sits there a while, and then is gone. Ah, see,
The divine afflatus leaves, and all's a-hush
Hawthorn calm as a sea.

4

Silence, it seems comes now...

The near-horizon bursts into flames and panoramic noises take
possession. The battle does not reach the poet, who, now in
moonlight, resumes. But this seems now of life rather than of
part of life: inspiration. Will it ever be finished?

4

This rock in the desert – is it protective, sound?
Beware, beware, such is no holy ground:
No rock is there, I think, to clasp and grasp
Because the sapient scorpion or the asp
Lie to its foot curled around.

5

Oh moon in a mist, how the dead reeds do grow!
Shells in a mist! Was it not ever so,
Since we all began, for us to climb the step?
Wars on the wind for ever, blow soft, blow low
Over my earthy deep.

Three Prison Sonnets

for Solita Solano

1

How long's a prisoner's day – long as an ell?
Not even a cigarette butt's in front of him,
The dusts and damps and mouldiwarps of Hell
Will see that that man's cup be full to the brim.
No more for him 'the darling buds of May',
All's the Hamletian gloom, now dark, now dim,
All's done, except 'Tomorrow's another day'…
It is indeed, and most of all for him.

Even God, they say, must suffer in this land,
Its cup past overflowing since how long?
As for poor Jesus, would he understand?
He would indeed, pain's sempiternal song.
And still alone, entombed, the prisoner sings
Awaiting dawn, until the welkin rings.

2

Of what does he dream, if such the case may be,
This damned prisoner in his accursed cell?
Maybe he dreams awhile of you and me,
And other unknown friends who wish him well,
Maybe dreams not. Of music dreameth he?
Dream on, sweet sleeper, an inch is worth an ell,
Catch it while cans't, while we unceasingly
Strive to undo, somehow, the locks of Hell.

When lovely sleep descends on thee at last,
I'll wager thou may'st dream of wanton girls,
Curled hair and snaky flank – of what unfurls
Beyond unseen horizons, possibly…

How good's all this, in jail's anatomy,
Despite 'Within it are ye helden fast'.

3

'Let not the divine afflatus gang agley,
Not in this minute no! Ah, how divine
Twould be could one but smoke and savour wine,
Such's not for us who long in prison lay,
Lie, and will doubtless lie...' a poet sings
One afternoon, until the welkin rings
(Ring soon, ring sweet, ring true). Maybe he faints
After these words addressed to all his saints.

What shall we do, all we who're not within
The barren, hapless cell, what can we *do*?
From what comes counsel? Tis nor me, or you
This death, this dust, they are not of our kin.
E'en music's useless, weeping mid its strings,
E'en April shaws and sound of freshnet springs.

By Their Faces Shall Ye Know Them

Look at their scowling faces, bless their hearts!
Here's Goya, most disgusted as we see,
And next, his father-in-law, the same as he,
More, even furious! And then again it starts
After Albeñiz, with the smaller fry:
That lovely marquess, that delicious king...
(Theirs not to think but merely pay and die),
And Balmes, young monk, and all the rest of the ring.
The thousands are more of a kind, less personal,
A sort of tapestry, of ox-cart wine –
And here's the architect, dear Rusiñol;

Alas for Romero de Torres – e'en he in his prime...
Wretched's the lot, in consternation, pain.
What's this about? The paper money of Spain.

In the Watches of the Night

In the watches of the night,
'When the stars are shining bright
And the winds are breathing low',
Say, oh say where shall I go!

In the reaches of the dark,
Is it 'hush' or is it 'hark' –
What am I that am not thee,
Jesus, Mary or Trinity?

In the stretches of high noon,
is it 'never' is it 'soon'?
World, pause awhile and let me be,
That am the path, the rill, the tree.

In the watches of the dawn,
What art thou but humble spawn,
When worm and louse ride over thee,
In the hollows of the sea,
And the dew corrodes the lawn?

Order

Like fighting one's way it is through a thick brick wall –
If the flower's at the end, then all may go right, go right –
Set never a time to this, nor 'now' nor 'night' –
But mark: 'If the tears must rise see that they do not fall.'

To Whom?

Into my arms in a cup of music, love,
That we may all pleasures prove and disprove
In an hour as iridescent as the dove
While our tears rise, fall not, but ever move
From clef to clef, out on the cliffs, my love –
The cliffs, the cliffs – that word comes from above,
Is sacrosanct. Nigeria has a grove
That seems to send for me. Hides this a trove,
An ancient treasure of men who died in love?
In heaven and earth are things that surely prove
Other philosophies than ours, my love;
Twas ever so – in times when the sea wove
Her turbulent arabesques, while the sun strove
To undo the moon, and failed as ever, and drove
New rages into time, from unanswered love –
So come with me that we the pleasures prove
And mate the query with its answering love.

Portrait-Sonnet

To be or not to be? *To be*, my heart,
Since whether he come at dawn or dusk of day
Love doth concede thee ever a flying start,
And truth goes with thee on thine errant way.
Despite the battle at the double gate,
Thou farest on apace, as all may see,
None can assess the meshes of thy fate,
Thy curious, wayward fate – well let it be!
O Primitif, moon-flecked, grass under dew,
Breeze-borne, by all the wandering spirits kissed,
O whippet-grace, O dreaming love-in-a-mist,
To thy own law thy allegiance solely due;
To thee, the dance, the music and the love –
To be, indeed – as thou dost hourly prove.

'Till Dawn do us Deliver'

To Clyde Robinson

'Till dawn do us deliver…' Down the ways
Of murderous history runs the masked phrase
Under wan moonlight murmured in prison days,
Alone and stark, or cupped in two lovers' hands,
Half threat, half promise – agonising both.
'Till dawn do us deliver…' Like an oath
A sigh, a moan, a scream, it says and unsays
All that has gone before – the flowers and seeds
That live and breed and rot, and all that bleeds
With eyes pressed to the stony heart of truth.
I think no word's so cruel as *Dawn*, forsooth,
Herald of yet more cruel days and ways;
The Devil stamps and Hell breaks out in praise –

(Of such can be our dawns on icy lawns).
Which would you rather: lone and feckless be
Or plunged within that sea of misery
UP to the brim, good heart, when the very lees
Climb to your throat? What says the heart? It dies?
'Till dawn do us deliver...' I surmise
You choose that love shall do as e'er it please
In its hard and cruel self, rather than desert be...
No thread's in this, of gold or sable strain,
Nothing's in this but night, night, night –
There's no surprise in this – I'll sonnet thee:

8 AM Sonnet

Look, here's a corpse at the holy foot of God!
5,503's his name; his hair was red,
Now he lies low upon the waiting sod,
Crumpled and empty on death's ready bed.
Will he do right by her, his sudden bride,
Loving her well, as every good man should,
Or will he turn himself on his left side
Eschewing all the pleasures of the blood?
The dawn came cold, but came at final last,
The executioners shivering in a ring,
The gong hung dumb and all the while how fast
An eyelid winked, as if to say '*Un*-bring
The order now – yes, now, now, now, now, *now* –'
Thus was all poised when Thomas broke his plow.

From Afar

The fire stirs, creeping afresh from the embers,
Dim is the light, sound died down, faded irretrievably.
I sit thinking of you, friends, partners of other times,
Gay, lusty, destitute and unsobered –
One hour's delirium
Beating innumerable wings through a web of forgetfulness.
What place is this for such phantasmagoria?
Do you not see I am estranged from you,
Going by new ways, spectator of elemental solitudes?
And on this eve
Now alone at the heart, a closed book that soon you must be
                                                    forgetting,
Even as I put your memorable gestures from me.

Of Liberty

I have sat by many fires and seen the leaves
Drift in the air, leaves parting from high trees
As thoughts run from a brain, when winters freeze
Outside, till wine is ripe in the flesh and weaves
Its restless determinations in the brain,
With here and there a flash of spirited gold.
Thoughts are stirred thus, fierce leaves against the skies,
Old tenants joyful, dragged from a haunted room
Where custom penned them in its relentless tomb;
Delivering winds come by, the prisoners fold
Free hands to speed the grateful prayers that rise
Soft as a smoke whose angry flame is out.

Then Freedom says: Thou shalt not speak of me –
I am the secret thing, the unexpressed
That fades to tremulous dust upon the breast

Of him that clasps and tells my history –
My name is you all, you shall not sing of me;
No banners swelling and no clarion's shout
To crown my phoenix, lest it burn again
To immortal ash. Say this alone of me:
The leaves stream in the skies, the winds are out.

Saintes De La Mer

They heard God's radiant voices in the deserts
Bidding them rise and northern countries seek;
Mary and Mary Salomé the meek
Set sail with fervent eyes to gain new converts,
Landed in wail of wind and weeping waves
Where the great Rhone breaks free – their holy graves
Are consecrate and hallowed. Nature's breath
Loosed on these savage sands now smoothes their dreams
In the stern tombs built for them, and at last
Their souls are freed from their religious fast,
Their saintly sorrows fled. Ah, true it seems
Earthly repose descends on these two fair
Adventurous saints, Saintes Maries de la Mer.

Aigues Mortes

The joyous centuries have gone as cloud
Slanting across immense and southern skies,
Borne on the mistral's violence, but the proud
Old town persists. Between four walls it lies,
Ramparts with fair commerce and tempestuous surge
Its giant shores. Such memories must be
The ghostly guards that watch each sun emerge
Out of the dying plain, and every night,
Worn with these windy battles, although dead,
Change medieval guard, give over fight
With time's modernity. Their eyes widespread
Marvel and mock at us; their last crusade
Is won in the endurance of their walls:
Aigues-Mortes their holy cross – and thus is made
The town impregnable, and silence falls.

Trasimene

Winter let out the herald day – a coil
Of roads swept down Cortona's hill to bring
Quick footsteps through the flushing February soil,
Where sombre Ossaio, built on misty ground,
Broods in the giant plain. A stream went round
Two full-blown toads that celebrated spring,
Pressing the easeful mud. White bulls were led
Curvetting in the dust, and the spring's mood
Rose in the veins of silent trees, and spread
Itself through fiery furrows in golden blood.
This plain has other bloods to fill its heart,
Where ghostly Punic bones rise to the keen
Haunting of owls, and the Roman legions start
Again by the shores of dolorous Trasimene.

When We Must Go Our Ways

When we must go our ways no more together,
After this shortening time that love has given
Our hearts to meet, remember that day of driven
And wayward rains, soft lulls in the wild weather,
And we on the road full-hearted, with mute lips
Masking the sorrow each should have of each
Once all things told. We saw the meadows reach
Wet arms about the river where it slips
To quietude and dies within the lake.
These waters where two swans wove silently
Their twin romance of summer's harmony
Heard your confession's ardour, saw us make
The delicate vow of love, though you are bound
Now on another quest, and faithfully
Go to its call; so from desire we found
Hope in the future's dear uncertainty.

The Solitary

And so I sit and let the hours pass
Huddled before the page and scarce awake;
In this deserted place there is no glass
To ring with mine, only still nights to slake
My thirsty craving with their lassitude.
And in the silence two caged birds are sleeping,
The fire is out, the hidden spiders creeping
Into the house along the rotting wood.
The very long complete decay of this
Spreading its tangled cobwebs to the noon!
A dusty cypress broods, this shanty is
Only a ravaged husk beneath the moon.
There is no sound inside, and by the dead

Embers of hearth my wingless thoughts are still,
Cradled in ashes; nothing stirs until
I hear life's maggot gnawing its last shred.

The White Cat

She moves in the rose alcove of this bed,
Secure, attentive to no vagrant lover
Whose claw annoys the latch; her senses bred
In warmth of dormant languors now discover,
As every night, a virgin paradise
Of seemly pillows, lucent napery,
Perpetual snow of linens that arise
To be explored, and singular tracery
Of hidden form – but in that moment she
Projects the utmost sapience of her ears
Across the silence, where a moth has cast
Unheeded farandoles of dusty tears
Courting the midnight oil, and wittily
Her paw arrests, and curls to sleep at last.

Or pensively she will unhood an eye,
A fiery bauble settled in the blue
Pernicious rim, that like a polar sky
Is cruellest of all colours; as the true
Too faithful pool that gave Narcissus joy
And death, this clear is her untempered look,
Remote as dawn – nor could a hand destroy
Her astral calm; and when the hand forsook
Its subtle flitting, coldly would she rise, –
Slow as a nun that fastens the first veil
Between her and the world, or diligent priest
That envies his own shadow yet dare not fail
By moribund faithless, shriving them with lies –
Or yearn, ancestral sphinx, towards the east?

Wansford Bridge Spring

Once more
Catkin and lambstail
In the landscape –
And on a black wind the quiver
Of pussy-willows –
And a swan's feather
On the grey river
Curling sea-ward.
Because of the wind in the north only these
Signs – and the black wind
Between us and Spring.

Looking at a Photograph in the Same Dress 1928 to 1926

I, like you then? No. Shadowy-seamed and old
My 1928...I change the theme
From self to lover – between the street and dream
Moves and delays our *now*. Arms that do fold
Your music within my reeds, and your eyes' arc
Actual or memorised, and dusky old
...Ah face, come dawn – Jealousy and the old dark
Afric we'll come to yet – These are the told
Numbers (and told again) our chart comports –
Lover, your servant I; and when the calms
Of seas incline to the real remoter palms
Down there, and timeless we shall rest or go,
Think then of, for us, on threshold of those ports:
All this, though dark, *was* ever – and tell me so.

For December

Haste, heart –
Eat, envy –
Neglect nothing.
Rhapsodise past rancours,
Yield, Ygdrasil.

Heart is honoured,
Envy eased,
Nothing love lacks –
Reunions, not partings – but break soon
Year, O bar athwart us.

Here we make a vow
Evenly for the two of us:
No miss nor loss of kiss –
Rule but, and time's to heel,
Yours, without years.

1929's Spring Poem

Why
Does Spring
Bloom these new little golden dead thistles
Empty snailshells
Papyrus-hued grass
Machine-made sample buds
In leather rubber cardboard ironware
Instead of
Steaming up and streaming down
Academically?

The Boeuf Blues

Back again between the odds and ends –
Back again between the odds and ends –
What once was gay's now sad,
What was unknown's now friends.

Each capital's not more than one Café
Wherein you lose (wherein you lose)
Yourself in what you have and have had...
Why worry choose, (why worry choose?)

The waiter waits, he will wait all night,
But when you're tight he will set you right
Back in tomorrow and even yesterday,
Time plays the piper, but what do we pay?

O Boeuf-sur-le-Toit, you had one song –
But when I look in the mirrors it all goes wrong.
Me-mo-ry Blues... and only back today...
    I'm a miserable travellin' man.

Equatorial Way

Not yet satisfied
But I'll be satisfied
With the days I've slaved for hopes,
Now I'm cuttin' all the ropes,
Gettin' in my due of dough
From ofays that'll miss me so –
Go-ing, Go-ing
Where the arrow points due South.

I don't mean your red neck farms,
I don't mean your Jim Crow trains,
I mean Gaboon –
I don't mean your cotton lands,
Ole stuff coons in Dixie bands,
I said Gaboon.
This ain't no white man's nigger,
Nor was – but I've grown bigger
The further away from you,
Further, longer away from you,
My cracker moon.

Doin' my own stuff now,
We know how to handle our niggers,
You-all's plumb crazy over there
Why, you might even let a nigger sit down with you,
Where'd we be if that happened?
Sure, that story of the gang to kill the firemen's true,
$25 a head we got for each dead nigger,
Killed 30 in Mississippi in a year,
Niggers gotta be kept in their place.
Tell you what's worse – that's them Northern whites
They just turn the niggers crazy, 'equality',
'Organise for better wages', 'black and white together fight'
Yah, we framed up
Angelo Herndon, gave him 20 years on the Georgia chain-gang
                                                              for that
Under pre-Abolition law, 'Incitement to slaves', not bad huh?
We hoped the 'Atlanta 6' bunch
Of whites and niggers with the same racket
Would get the death penalty. Sure, we always let the
Mobs take the prisoners unless we
Shoot 'em ourselves; that was the Tuscaloosa lot,
Weren't no gang of masked men at all,
Did it ourselves, yah, quick and neat
Save the third boy didn't die – oh that's alright
Daren't testify 'gainst no-one, we beat 'em in jail

Beat their families too, make 'em sign
'Under duress' we calls it. They sign, don't ask no help
From outside, perfec'ly content with lawyers court gives 'em.
We run them International Labor Defense attorneys out the town,
They nigh got lynched on the train, huh.
Know what them agitators for 'Equal Rights' is askin'?
'Self-determination for the Black Belt'.
Well, farmer over there'll show you an old lynched nigger's tooth.
Kinda lucky he thinks, on his fob,
Holds it up when a cropper hands him sauce
Askin' fer wages...
That's the kind o' 'Self-determination' we got,
Don't need no interference,
That's why we're shooting so many niggers jes' now,
Ain't we gotta protec' our white women?
Naw, ain't no rape, why a nigger wouldn't dare...
Jes' our word, sorta slogan.
Old nigger in Maryland, Euel Lee, in jail 3 years now
Fer nuthin – farmer and fam'ly found murdered,
Course he didn' do it, that nigger asked for his wages
See? cain't have that; other niggers would too.
Them Scottsboro boys is innocent, we all knows that –
But hell, looka what'd happen if they free 'em...
Other niggers 'd be asking for their rights,
Showin' how we keep 'em on chain-gangs till they die,
Share-croppers goin' to planters for pay,

Equator, Pole and Pole –
Fixin' to board the prow
And let the ocean roll and roll
And roll me over, even,
To where the Congo waters roll.

Won't take from the old lands
But twelve bottles of gin –
Won't leave on the old lands
But my cheque cashed in –

Then make clear to the Black Folks
They can't but win.

Last advice to the crackers:
Bake *your own* white meat –
Last advice to the lynchers:
Hang *your brother* by the feet.
One sitting pretty black man
Is a million strong on heat.

Goin' to beat up Fear on the octaves,
Tear the cracker limb from limb –
Goin' to take on each-every vengeance,
Drum one blood-blasting hymn –
And laugh, laugh, laugh in the shadows,
Louder'n Death – I'll be watching him.

Southern Sheriff

White folks don't kill each other in the South
Ho no, not with so many niggers around.
It's the wrong end of the stick you got, englishman.
You say: 'here's a murder, find the criminal'
We say: 'too many niggers around with uppity ideas'
So we jus' take one or two along for murder,
Oh we ain' p'ticlder, don't have to be no corpse
Found, we arrest 'em 'for vagrancy', on suspicion-like,
We *frame* 'em, yah. Say, didn' Governor Sterling of Texas say
Sometimes you gotta burn a house to save a village?
That's when that nigger was framed
(Governor said mighta been innocent,
But a white woman cain't lie, see?)
Rape? sure they rape white women,
Leas'ways they'd like to – that's good enough.

Askin' for unemployment insurance;
Might git together with the poor-whites
More'n they do – yah, we been breakin' up those meetings –
Askin' fer 'probes an' enquiries',
An', well, tryin' to stop all we do,
Because we gotta protec' our bosses ain't we?
Why, it'd upset the whole South.
Now the Ku Klux Klan
Weren't made fer nuthin' I suppose?
And if we don't get lynch *law* we have plain lynchin'.
We got ex-Senator Heflin
Knows how to talk:
'If Alabama courts can't
Stop nigger rapists white men can and will.'
Whole case been goin' on too long,
Whole world protestin',
Oughta had 'the quickest way out', courts is too slow.
Reckon *we* can account fer about 80 niggers we killed this year,
Right here in Birmingham, Alabama – year ain't over yet:
Tisn't everyone knows that,
We got our records, from Jan. to Aug., 'bout 80 niggers.
An' we'd like to shoot every son of a bitch that comes down here
Talking 'equal rights' – them white agitators
And niggers from the North.
Maybe we'll get to doin' it.
Only thing is
Looks to me they're gettin' more and more determined,
Those that calls themselves 'comrades',
Gettin' an' stickin' together,
Jes' won't do if it goes on...

That is the Southern justice,
Not lynch-mobs, but part of the Law speaking.

'Rape'

To Haywood Patterson

A small farmer's wife speaking

'Here's that hot rain again
Makin' the Georgia earth so red…
They say it's niggers' blood made it red first,
Huh, the damn niggers groanin' an' bellyachin' –
When I go out they don' seem to see me no more
Like they used to – even Mandy's kinda queer,
They don' pray so much, that's it –
They's secret, quite a pack o' them's evil;
I guess it'll pass, when cotton and cane's right again.
Most cain't read – what they know 'bout 'world crisis'?
(An' what the hell's that to *us*?)

Well, I 'member *Uncle Tom*
An' how the slavers got sold up,
An' that sorta peachy wife in the middle of the book…
(Feelin' kinda soft today myself too,
An' no one 'round) –
What they grumble about now they're *free*,
What more they want? Ain' we had to swallow
The Yank's meddlin?
Granpa said… Oh to hell with Granpa,
We're sick of our men – anyway that part's right
In that paper from the North,
Sick of them mostly.

Well, the storm's here now…
An' what's a Communist?
An' what's a 'peon'? Wish I knew.
Suppose I asked that new nigger there with the pigs…
Sumpthin' like: come in an' tell me, nigger,
Did *you* help make this earth so red?

Don't see no blood gone outa you, no –
Kinda handsome too... ugly black... looka them shoulders,
Wow... an' them ham-hands messin' up pigs' food...
Wonder what it's like to...
Well? Mebbe yeah... Ain't the house empty?

'Comme here nigger, say,
Wanta ask you sumpthin'...
Damn fool's deaf – Here nigger,
What's your name, ain't seen you 'bout the place before,
Who's your master right now?'
'Massah? Massah boss...'
'Why ma'am, yuh fo' sure'.
'Aw come in nigger, don't matter 'bout your name,
You're mine, see? Don't be scared,
That there's the rain, not white menfolks
Stompin' about the house.
I'm 'lone today, see? I'll treat you good
If you talk to me, git a little frien'ly,
I kinda likes you.
Say, what's a Communist – heard you bin having some 'roun
                                         these parts –
What do they do? And what's a 'peon'?
You're free, ain' you, though you're mine too, see?
Becos we protec' you-all, we like your folk,
But you don' seem grateful no more...
Jes' won't answer, huh?
Mebbe you got sumpthin' to teach me
An' I'm a white woman, see?
Thinka that, alone with a big black nigger...
Well, you got sumpthin' to show me then?
Come on, nigger, I'll say you gotta give it me...
You damn nigger beast... you won't?
Well, you raped me anyhow...
We-all know niggers jes' gotta rape white women –
Looka that! Jumped clean outa the back door! An' his name's Roly,
Hick Roly, I knowed it all along –

Your number's up, Roly
Git what's comin to you…'

So they took the dogs out, the bloodhounds, an hour later when
                                          the men were back,
And they cotched him in the swamps
And what the hounds left they hung on a tree
And plugged it plumb full
And the guns were hot with shooting at it,
And so they went home,
And the lady of the house was honoured,
And they had the moonshine out,
'Weren't much of a nigger,
Already half drowned hisself tryin' to git away,
Not much fight left.'
And the farmer said: 'Well, goddam,
'Nother nigger ter find fer them pigs,
Not so hahd these days, go git one from camp,
Guess warden owes me sumpthin' for that las' keg –
Ain't going' to be no fuss about this black stiff,
Jes' a mess o' black pieces in the swamp,
Foot-loose nigger ennyway till I took him,
Nobody's nigger.'

And that was just one more lynching that year
Among the 48 in 1933.

Réanville

For Hadley

Moth and cheese and rust and dung –
(Oh Paris, Paris, Normandy –)
The wordless smell, the curtain hung

Across the years, the five gone by
Under the Boot – the while you play
With myth and moth, and snake, and smell
The unaccounted lactic strain
Rise, music-like, from every fold
That kept the Mowrers from the cold
Such hours they burned their midnight oil
Bent over Teuton deviltry –
I, in French, savage village-cot
Am aureoled with dust and dung
Imbuing now the shining words
Of poets – laid, now cold, now hot
On print, MSS, and letter-love
And twenty years of paper there.
Here is a bead, a mask, a hair
I wore, before the men were shot
In Badajoz, Guernika bombed,
And later thousands felled, entombed
All in a day, now here, now there,
Throughout the world, the roaring world…

Dung is more quiet, French-made dung
Of peasants, laid quite carefully
Upon your book and mine, and left
Till, after months, it have become
part of the book, the history
Of all the world, and you and me –
(And, who can tell, become the key
Of what, though plain, seems mystery…)

'Death to the intellect' was roared –
These Norman peasants heard the cry
And oped their breeches and let fly.
The Germans only burned the books,
And played their war and went away –
The peasants shat another day.

And while you shook the curtains yet,

My past, it rose in one great wave,
One giant hour of forty years
Laid flat, ten deep, upon the floor –
And regal rust shone here and there
As sunlight will upon the hair,
And 'bit at foot upon the stair...

No more, no more, NO MORE for me –
For you the curtains shaken clean
Of all the stuff of 'would have been
Were it not thus' – but here the hell
Come clean at last, and that race run...

[unreadable], grüss-gott! *My* garden's green,
All's well withal – the war's begun!

In the Studio

Is it March, spring, winter, autumn, twilight, noon
Told in this distant sound of cuckoo clocks?
Sunday it is – five lilies in a swoon
Decay against your wall, aggressive flocks
Of alley-starlings aggravate a mood.
The rain drops pensively. 'If one could paint,
Combine the abstract with a certain rude
Individual form, knot passion with restraint...
If one could use the murk that fills a brain
Undo old symbols and beget again
Fresh meaning on dead emblem...' so one lies
Here timeless, while the lilies' withering skin
Attests the hours, and rain sweeps from the skies;
The bird sits on the chimney, looking in.

In San Gimignano

For Ernesto Ferri, Musician

On such a day in the *doce* and *trece*
Others too will have run to that window crying out
'Look, look! Here's all Tuscany blotted with rain,
With mists and a tiny snow... Look!
All Tuscany's here in a cup of guesses,
In a hood of vision and memory – the proof and the promise.'

'Music', said you, '*what* is music?', you ask me the *meaning* of music!
Surely if such were knowable it would be something like madness..."
I am sure of your words, Ernesto Ferri, that day.
(The *meaning* of music – who would think of such a thing but
myself?)
But now I am thinking of Dante
On the fabled bridge, of his meeting there with Beatrice;
Yes – and what, do you suppose, is the *meaning* of love?
How many years have I not thought of this – maybe all life itself –
Of Dante's meeting, or fabled meeting, on that bridge...
Of the vast Italian landscapes with their secrets between the
mountains,
The towers and flowers, and the Spring that comes like a giant,
'Eccome qua', all in an hour...
Of the toads in their clutch of love, the bull led out curvetting,
Cortona's masterly spring –
Thinking of the plains and rains, of the wars and the Medioevo,
And Ossoia ('a place of bones') and Urbino's *Ostia*,
Mysterious, eaten heart, by sublimely-perspective Uccello.

Here with a surge like Giant Spring in his hour,
In the cold curve of winter (that is a point to make)
Ernesto Ferri seizes my hands and shouts
'Look! Look with me at all of this!' and we run to the window,
And all we see is mist, yet all we know is there
Cupped and sealed in its coffer of future splendours:

The springs and Mays and morns, in the slender, icy rain
Or snow would it be?) – silent strength in the silent greyness,
Hushed and remote, all the towers taut in the air,
Frozen and fisted.
                    (Ah me, San Gimignano,
Mai piu, mai piu, mai piu – yet why do I write '*mai piu*'?
Must I break into wars, Ernesto, and conjugate their tenses
That say *Mai piu, mai piu* – fading out of a '*chi lo sa*'?)
                    (Oh be this '*chi lo sa*' today my guerdon,
                    (Oh be this '*chi lo sa*' our sorrow's guardian.)

     That day
You played, oh how you played without your violin…
You began with Shelley,
Your words soared into poems and the hands of your *maestria*
Lept to the corals on my throat, and you touched them
(As did your Aldo), saying it would bring us luck,
Luck to all three, if we could but just *toccare*
The lovely 'horallo' together, and this, all three, we did.
     (Meanings live here, it seems, undreamed elsewhere.)

Now, later, I find some eyes that are surely Sienna's
As limned by the lovely Nelli and his peers in that early time
Such craftsmen have told the story, the poem of cheek and eyelash
Where they come together – and Giotto, with his cowl on the
                                                    perfect line…
Italy, Italy!
Trampled, resurgent, remembered and pressed to breast,
Like one of the surges in Swinburne, flame-filled in an ice of
                                                    waiting,
Till the time shall come for the freeing, and now that time is
                                                    expressed!
Ernesto Ferri, *salute!* I will soon doff my Swinburne
And turn to the sonnet form, and the earlier, sheerer way;
Look, passionate Galleotti is peaking to Dante,
All love's told in two lines: 'We read no further that day',
'That day we read no further.'

Such, yes, is the *maestria* of poetry: all love told in six words:
'Quel giorno non leggemmo piu avanti',
With three or four lines before to fill the stage:
A man, a woman, a book – there is not even a tankard
Mentioned to quicken the colour and heighten the pulse and rhythm;
Maybe it was there all the same, tankard before the dagger...

   You would play that well, very well indeed, I think
   Ernesto Ferri.

June for Italy – June For Freedom

Letter to the Poet Gawsworth most actively there

Then up spoke June 11 on the air;
'Pursuit...out of Roman country... entering Tuscany now.'

Half Italy's freed! Tarquinia's safe,
Stone man and woman on the tombs keep their Etruscan *status quo*
Viterbo passed (great dome monumented in memory);
What of Orvieto, Signorelli's Crack of Doom on the great holy
           walls there?
Grosseto... Orbetello – flowering meads and water flats –
Mars finding foot heavy to run with here...mocked by bull-frogs?
Inland: Spóleto... Montefalco,

  (Message for AMG:
  The Gozzolis here
  Were in very good condition
  On their little round hill,
  One of those Benozzo did so often
  In his frescos incorporate.)

Map? In the heart's eye only – no other.

Gubbio, it says, Gubbio and the Podestá's magnificent castle;
Castagni e noci throughout the land here I think,
Maize is festoons on each house, come autumn, for the people's
                                                            polenta,
(*And for mine too*, once more.)

Arezzo? Let Cosroe fight on round the story of the True Cross
Sabre high, battle-axe, masterful headgear, flowering horses;
Piero Francesca painted it, the great mélée of spears and faces.
Borgo San Sepolcro- here Signorelli's austere pain in the Crucifixion.

I remember 'u(m)briaco in Umbria', with the wine almost black,
And how, in one hour, the winter snapped on a hill
And the waters rushed out of Cortona, and Spring said: N o w!
Immensely flushed the plain, quilt and symphony
Pricked out with vines and flowers... Ossoia here,
A Roman time of bones – Trasymene.
San Gimignano – towers, Dante, Benozzo –
Siena of the blue hills, purple, volcanic Volterra.

        Send news, send news! –
Of Urbino and the Duke of the Nose and Warts;
San Marino, Rimini, Ravenna,
Bologna, Ferrara... tutti cuanti, tutti cuanti right up to the Lakes.
Orcagna and Gozzoli,
Piero della Francesca and
(Bramantino)
Suardi,
        Stay safe.

After the plan made, the drink in council taken, the feet singing
                                                together as they go:
March – March March – March March – March March –
                                        March March – March,
            Neatly and strongly
            O N.

Fuori i Tedeschi And down with the Fascists!

Kikuyu

More and more black must the blood run?
Chains tighter round your limbs be strung,
Where some are shot and others hung...
What price all this, since all's begun?
        Kikuyu, Kikuyu, Kikuyu.

'I see a world without a slave':
These words may seal our century's grave.
Aim at the heart, both spend and save
All – now the sign's come oer the wave,
        Visez le ccoeur.

Force stored for spending. Thus prepare,
Cool head, hot heart. The sign? Tis air!
Much premature? Ye here, my dear,
It comes across the wave from there,
        Arrow to heart.

Visez le coeur. Who stoned the wind,
That fifty-fifty kind-unkind
Co-traveller? Time out of mind
Twas thee, twas I that stoned the wind.
        Now shoot for the heart.

Si tout dévale et tout s'en va,
Les temps hésitent à mettre bas
Leur monstres, un çi et l'autre là;
Rien n'est fini – d'accord sur cela?
        Tirez au coeur.

Jaime

'Here go I but for the grace of God'
Are words as old as true – and what I see

Is this mysterious shape in front of me,
That is nor man, nor eft, nor stone, nor clod –
A cripple, ay, for all eternity.
Nought can repair, nought can restore this thing
Framed by some sudden fit of infancy,
Nor love nor hate, nor devil, king,
Parliament, system, science, not even spring;
All's done and lost, because of destiny.

It drags itself along as best it may
In street and bar; some gape and others sneer
At this small mess of bones sprawled on the floor
That's lifted up while onto a chair
That it with you may pass the time of day.
It utters curious sounds – they're words, I swear.

Fine head, fine hands – the rest's a raggle of pain,
A higgle-piggle of broken spillikins
Linked by the snakes. (Indeed the devil wins
Outright, for ever, thus.) It says its name,
(A phantom, it seems, has that, if spawned here):
'I'm Jaime, Meorquín'. You like his game?
(If game it be). My Lords, this too is Spain.

Late Night Sonnet

For Clyde Robinson, American

'Echo on echo runs into the past,
Ply over ply the serried memories
Lie on the shore, from bitter first to last,
No one-time rose that bloomed but ever dies...'

'Come now: Was all of life such a cursed thing,

All of it blasts and gales and fearsome rain,
None of it August-rose, all grudging spring?
Come now, look back, think hard, and look again:
Was most of it a questing from here to Mars,
And all the rest a mass of shards and spars,
And broken loves, and all the rest of that,
All of it cold, all in 'the rage of Mart'?'
'Not all, not all, not only – Once I sat
Close to the heat of Spanish hearth and heart.'

Letter

For, and to, John Hayward, From N.

It's ELIOT now who's dead – says the lunch-time Radio here,
                              half-heard because of the usual clatter
of forks on plates,
The interruptive chatter…

Eliot

We met, you and I, first, that summer night of 1922,
At a ball – You in 'smoking', I in a panniered dress
Of Poiret: red, gold with cascading white tulle on the hips.
The P. of W. was there (so polite, lovely face) and we danced
                                                    together;
The hostess, that small termagent, in all her glitterings,
Brilliant was she, the hostess, at this sort of thing.

Bored by it all was I. After many dances we went down
Alone, by the grand staircase to the supper room.
It was *then*; Eliot, you came in, alone too, for the first time to my
                                                          eyes;
Well-advised of you was I, already somewhat versed in you:
I mean *Prufrock*.

This *Prufrock* of yours, in 1917,
Was given to me by an Irish officer.
I think he had the stamp of the poet too,
Else would he have loved it so well? From that day on,
He (my first lover since marriage) and you came together…
Gratuitous, fortuitious, this linking, one well may say.
Such things make a 'complex'. It is magic.
Thank you, Eliot. It lasted what *I*, in life, have had to call 'a long
time';
The lover, in Flanders fighting till he was killed there: 9 months.
Prufrock remained, with its sayings, those then my dirge.
In all, your *Prufrock*, it got into my fibre,
Not only because of itself but because, of the way it came to me.
I never told you this, oh never, never.
Seized was I by your looks, your way, your eyes, at that ball:
'The solitary eagle', I said, 'that is it, that is you.'

We were alone in that vainglorious room,
Both of us thinking 'Much can be talked about,
It seems.' *And so it was*, despite others coming in,
For perhaps two hours on end and maybe more,
About, about, what about? Nor you, nor I
Could now recall – champagne and lobster well to hand.
So entranced was I by you I suggested 'a tryst'
For the next night. You certainly came to it.

Restaurant Eiffel Tower, Percy Street, London in what was
known as The Wyndham Lewis Room
Tough the painting there was all by 'Bobbie Roberts'.
You, pale, restrained, impassive – I suppose these could be three
words.
We had been invited to dinner, both, by the Hutchinsons;
I begged you not to get us there, and in the end I won.
So, by the little gas fire, on the floor, we lengthily sat.
Our talk, it seemed to be going on so long,
That Joe, the Tower's Austrian waiter, came up to see,
Found us by that heat (cold evening) as close as could be:

'Want anything?' said Joe, smiling at me.
'More gin, Joe, please, make it doubles same as before.'
Eliot went on talking while I admired his gradual unthawing.
What *can* we have talked about so concentratedly?
Metaphysics? Psychology? The hither-and-yons of life?
Sitting on that small floor, imbibing Gin-Philosophy... *Not*
                                        Gin-Philosophy only.
Of the dinner itself I remember nothing at all,
Save that we two were there, and just we two.
(Do *you* remember *everything* that's happened to you?) And then?
Not every life-moment's recalled, though all of that night
                                        certainly is...
Not every moment goes into one's histories,
Be they written, or even, spoken.

Ara Vos Prec – Then *The Waste Land*
It put its rightful frenzy into me.
I do not understand it yet, nor ever shall
Reach its full import, its span, its entirety.
(For one who's obtuse, most times, and that is me,
Count me well in.)
It changed, however, my life in its own time,
As it has changed the lives of poets in many lands.
Indeed, I am one of these too.
Is it passion and repression, repression as well as passion?
Yourself, aureoled with visions and with echoes,
That is clear, and also with chosen, well-tried allusions,
But the soul of it all is a mystery to me.
So be it. See, Eliot, how not fully understanding, one can love a
                                        thing,
Full far from one's own ways, yet the 'self-of-it' held close?
            But why *repressions*?

    This sort of thing, maybe, we talked about, so close to that
                                        good gas fire,
I think I must have said: 'But why repressions?'
This was some time before *The Waste Land* came out.

Ah, you're a great poet – no mistake about that whatever;
Your progressions, digressions, and the kiss of rhyme on rhyme,
Sure technique, the slopings of metre into metre,
The ferryings from rhythm to rhythm.
    I do not think you are a 'depressive' poet, Eliot,
Nor that you were ever an 'encouraging' poet either,
Save because of the very beauty of your lines.
But what's 'Encouragement'? No rising poet needs that in mind:
Find out for himself he will, the stuff of his own kind.

Great is my love for *The Waste Land*: for those 'Terres en Friche',
Or do you prefer 'Terre de Friche', or, even, 'Terrains Vagues'?
'Die Wüste' in German. 'La Yerma', that is in Spanish…
Whichever, great gold is there, throughout all of it.

    Straw Men, as well. With, also, your *Gerontion*.

    And here, I stop. *He dicho.* I have done.

(Save to salute you, from distance across the years…
Who should look for the obvious rhyme that could follow here:
                                                            Tears?)

Lincoln

'My paramount object is to save the Union, and not to either save
or destroy slavery.'

'If I could save the Union without freeing any slave, I would do it.
If I could save it by freeing all the slaves, I would do it. And if I
could do it by freeing some and leaving others along, I would also
do that.' (From a letter to Horace Greely, 1862)

'I can now most solemnly assert that I did all in my judgement

that could be done to restore the Union without interfering with
the institution of slavery. We failed, and the blow at slavery was
struck!' (From 'Life, Public Services and State Papers of Abraham
Lincoln'.)

> If I could free the Union... so it went
> Down Lincoln's pen... I'd free the slaves, yet not
> For their but Union's sake, if freeing meant
> The Union be kept whole; again, I'd *not*
> Agree to freeing if *that* saved the Union;
> Third plan: free some, leave others as they are
> To save... Thus straddled in perplexed communion
> He spawned his insult 'free'. They put bar
> Before, behind, longsides, athwart the black
> In reassertion of his branded back,
> And Lincoln's grinding verbiage dressed that lie
> From then till Lenin, and the black man said
> Nuthin' or handled death – until our cry:
> 'My love, my friend, my comrade – black on red.'

The Love Story

> The time for fairy-tales is past; secure
> The latch was shut on children's dreams, but one
> Escaped, and daring fled into the world,
> Where growing magically men called it Love.
> In secret hurrying through the troubled nights,
> Like feverish criminals that fear pursuit,
> We hide the gold of our discovery,
> Trembling to look on it. Ah, where shall be
> Time for the heart to rest and hands to hold
> Untrembling all the treasure, breath be found
> To conjure into life this stolen gain
> And clasp it, willing fellow, to our joy?

The shining bird that will not be constrained
Nor tamed with dazzling toys, the lightning flame
That strikes and shatters, the fiery paradox
That burns the soul into sobbing sea
When all is done and the sweet story fled –
Then grow we old and weary of all tales.

¿Me Oyes, Mijito?

To Arturo Gardoqui

Una noche del Amaya
With the beefsteak on its plate,
And the Araucano ripe, round, and gorgeous – the Indian fast on
                                          the setting sun –
Una noche del Amaya, (¿Donde mi hombre, donde mi hombre?)
Una noche del Amaya
Between the drinks and the scorn and the drunken,
The peppery piece and hand stretched to tear your cap off...
Ah how they come and go here (¿but adonde mi hombre?)
Una noche del Amaya – what am I trying to say?

'They believe in *the heart* in Chile, believe in using it'
Someone opined, and I looked at my plate,
Saw a heart there – mine, I think – said 'I will eat it',
And eating it '¿Donde mi hombre, donde mi hombre?'

Temper is free in Chile, at least there is that,
And so, you Celts of many lands, this is the place for you.
Vital and total extremes are in honour in Chile,
Not only in honour but practised... (but ¿adonde mi hombre?)
I continue to eat my heart; it has gone cold on the plat,
And I remember: temper is incidental here, if accidental...

The world over
Men sleep under bridges,
Men in the once-sined shoe, men in the Stetson hat;
But here my lover sleeps 'not even under bridges',
Sleeps full of wine, poems and ire (Ah ¿adonde mi hombre?)
And I, why am I here and not under those 'not even bridges',
Why am I here? Would I were there at this hour.
Under a bridge, is it? Also beyond the waters of firmament,
There dwells my man (for a flood to tell it as quake has told it).

The heart, the heart on the plate, after it turns tough and cold,
After you've ate of it fills again, grows never too old –
But *whose*? Ay that's the question.
Will you come and eat a cut of heart with me,
Drunkard, my drunkard? We can sit down to a good piece of it,
                                                            you and I,
Sleep all the sweeter after 'under the bridges', mijito…

Oh let us go
From the Amayan fumes to a Solutrian silence,
To where the secular Phoebus spends his rays
Playing at God yet where the Indians laid
Stone upon century; I would like such days
With you between those ruins, before all gets waylaid.

Having gold I place it upon my knee;
I thread my gold, and then my gold leaves me.
                        (Coming out of sleep with these lines)

Mosley 1943

Fascism incarnate, Britain's. This
Is Mosley, undenied, forthright,
And out of jail. This paradox
Invites three million men to fight.

How will it work, this non-pareil
Of treachery? Though your tacking's right,
You'll need Excalibur, Morrison,
To prick three million souls to fight.

Should we invoke our allies' shock?
Ay, but its first the Briton's right:
Aren't we enough to ask if you
Dare ask three millions hearts to fight?

Does not the Army say 'Thumbs down',
And Air and Sea shout back the same?
What say the dead? Safe dead they jeer
'For this we fought, to save *this* game!'

And all of us, with plough or pen,
That win the coal or fish the sea,
Or drive the lathes must feel *Down tools…*
D'you really want such things to be?

Down tools? No, for that's Hitler's wish.
This is our war, nor shall we fail
If every factory hammer rings:
Mosley must go back to jail.

Thank you: folks sleep in Tube tonight
Because of Mosley's master's way.
How many more will sleep in camps
All concentrate, come Mosley's day?

The people's instinct does not fail,
And back of instinct in this case
The proofs are shored since '31
Of Mosley beastly acts, and face.

Have you forgot Olympia and
Black Sunday in hot ripe East End?

Prove black is white, you'd have to, as
When Mosley says he's 'Britain's friend'.

We are a true and honest race,
Able, not stupid, generous, brave,
When men like you will let us be:
Can you make hero mate to knave?

Can you deny heroes exist
And martyrs too, since that first day?
But this is a very dirty war
If you can swing things in this way.

I know, you'll say: 'The premise? False.
We think of future moves; it's chess;
Mosley is unimportant, to...'
Official angle on this mess.

All this, far more than straw in wind
Suggests the kind of peace ahead,
And yet, remember: cup-lip-slip...
May Britain be worthy of her dead.

Myself

I am alone,
Sitting in the proverbial deserted country
Unmoved by this recurrent fantasmagoria
Of public holidays – here in this early August
Antagonised by life, not to be drawn
From the secluded alchemy
Of contemplation. True, there have been many hours
When I have longed for wine and with it those conversations
Reverting to the metaphysical, a lure

That sets the mind on the old pinnacle
Which I have likened to the balancing
Of jugglers' knives – but that is past,
And what is past is vastly better to me
Than the florescence of some banal future
I cannot govern.
                         Here am I
Today in my sundress, smiling, obstinate,
And I am reading seriously – how Mme de Stael
Thought that the human race was capable of perfection
And disagreeing with her – (for we have all ideas
Founded on various things about perfection).
Reading how Mme de Stael liked politics
And was romantic all through the Revolution.
Here the wind blows and cigarettes are mingled
Through the long day with vagrant meditations;
The garden is full of green apples
That I shall never pick. In the evening
I lie in a large field and think of Africa
Teeming with animals, dream of its spaces and mysteries,
Later return unhaunted
By the day into the creaking, haunted house.
I am alone and careless, sometimes troubled
By a strange dream of shipwrecks where the sea
Has swallowed legions, bearing me up
On a wave of salt, I disconcerted
By this strange, deferential trick of fate,
A solitary survivor.
                         'Et je suis veule...'
                              forbidding phrases
Fall through the mind like the fall of the green, hard apples,
And the grey garden is empty of flowers. These synonyms
I have not looked for but were pressed on me,
I the tramp of London knowing all the night-watches,
Now dreaming for pleasure to come out of the month of August
Once back in the spotted country, pleasure mingled
With the tossing of grasses, the flush of the harvested hay crops,

The wink of a daisy when my guests depart through the wicket.
(Guests of a moment) so that I may return
To the perusal of the French language and lesser poetry.

These hours pass nameless and unperceived; meanwhile
In the offing swings a purple buddleia
Flicking away the propositions of the future.

And an Afternoon

Sitting in Lyons, sitting in Lyons,
Lyons is London, Lyons is not the world,
Is London Lyons? London is not the world…
Tra-ra, light-headed a little, in a little Lyons.
I feel as if Greater Time Street were round this corner
Leading to a *Place* called 'World', la Place du Monde.
It has a guillotine in the centre and may do a long time yet.
Do you wait to get there from here, and is it possible, and who
                                                              are we?

'I think I'll love you, Morris, till I die'
(And when is that, and what is 'love', and who are you?
Tra-ra, a little ligh-headed.)
Tomorrow we will have music; tomorrow, my Morris,
Shake the old nebulae out of Time's windy sack,
But today let me sit in silence, as in all those 4 AMs one sat
In Montmartre, between music and daylight suspended,
Wondering about 'meaning', well away in that labyrinth with
                                                    echoes for guides…

No, London is not Lyons – or else I am not alive…
I'll ever love you if I loved you ever –

This was a moment between snow and tea, and I
A hand on a pencil moving, eye half shut…

And Lyons: Self-Service, Take Your Tray, Move On:
At six P M it closes.
    Oh fierce and sharp and sweet
    The great, plain wind outside, telling the traveller,
    '*All* is not lost.'

April, 1942

Black out the world, Shakespeare's in a grave,
And Dickens-heart-by Thames, and summer-full Chaucer;
War's in his heaven, sorrow in exelsis, lovers asunder –
Nought but a grudging spring
Have we this day and Chaucer who says it best:

    'The slayer of himself yet saw I there,
    His herte-blood had bathed all his hair:
    The nayl y-driven in the skull at night;
    The colde death, with mouth gayping upright.
    In midst of all the temple sat meschaunce,
    With sory comfort and evil countynaune.
    Ther I saw madness laughying in his rage,
    Armed complaint, alarm and fierce outrage.
    The body in the bushe, with throte y-bled,
    A thousand slayne, and none of sickness dead;
    The tiraunt, with the prey bi-force y-refte;
    Ther burnt the shippes daunsying up and down;
    Ther dyed the hunter by the wilde lion:
    The sow eating the child right in the cradle;
    The cook y-skalded, for all his longe ladel.
    Nought was forgot the ill-fortune of Mart:
    The carter over-ridden by his cart,
    Under the wheel full lowe he lay adoun.'

To the wars he was a hole packed of years, Dan Chaucer.

Saturday Night in 'The Golden Lion'

For Nina Hamnett

Fine as a fresco the face stands out,
Six-deep, ten-deep faces exactly framing it each side –
A beer and a broad smile –
Pallor mated with darkness. Is it Slav or is it Latin?
The beret tops the whole, *surnage la compagnie.*
Six foot something, beautiful face, framed with profiles.
Cettinje? Cross of Australasia? Would a scientist know?
(God, what a world it can all be when…but no, it's not time yet.)
Beer and a broad smile (How simple it all is, when it is.)
This man has the physique of what I mean when I say: comrade,
And, possibly, the heart.

A hand comes up to affirm the *bon bock.*
So that's the kind of hand it is, is it – hence the kind of man,
A working hand, untroubled with equivocations;
Tells me 'One does what one has to do',
And 'What one's going to do.'

I wasn't thinking I'd ever see that face again,
And then, a month later, in the same place:
'I am a Red Indian', he said, 'Red Indian from Canada.'
There you are Britain, there's our today of Allies.

October–November Night in 'The Coach & Horses'

Coal fires – autumn, bedamn, is it, with the leaves down?
You wouldn't have noticed it, no, we're so all of a piece here now
    with time and the way things are and the weather,
In the desert of waiting.
Fetch a sigh an' you will – the radio bubbles on:
'America's expenditure' – what's yours? what's mine?
Mine's income tax – what's yours?
And here's your heartache in the corner where it's always been.

Who are you talking to? Myself of course,
Yet the time of vacant shuttles weave the wind is dead
(And wasn't it long, and true?)
Here's a coal for the fire – and fire in the coal, bedamn.
That cuts both ways…No, that cuts four ways…
What does? I've forgotten. You'd better forget it. Drunk again?
Not so's you'd notice. Here's the pep talk on.

As it proceeds I hear a different strain:
'Black troops aren't *allies*, are *subjects*,
An' a subjec', he pushes a wheel; he can' draw up no report – '
'What you talkin' about buddy?'
'De *British* black man's *an ally*, Dis war make it so.
De *British* black folks claims deir *British* rights, and though
Plenty British say his wrong, plenty more say it right be so.'

Sounds like a pub-full of people –
Of course it does – that's exactly what I am;
That is, part of me is.

And all in all, murk, black-out conquers nerves?
And all in all, who's best off, Europe or you?
And by and large, the muddlers'll muddle through?
Expect they will, old man.
    Waiting, waiting, waiting – oh waiting.
And then, OH THEN, it bursts, in North Africa,
It begins to come true.

Of a Glass Stopper Found in the Sea at Collioure S.W. France, in 1951

To Valentine Ackland, with the stopper

How old is this glass stopper, tunred
Into that something ripe and strange
By wave and sand in their sea-change,
Their velvet wash upon Collioure,
While time crept on five hundred years,
Or flamed in one decade of wars
(My own scored there by Spanish tears)?
Gods of those seas might know, won't tell,
No arrogant unborn be sure.

Pisces Pulled Plough

(Hardest of all in the arduous February days)

'Tired? No, *exhausted*, but far more indignant still,
We the two Fishes' (they said) 'That were wont to fill her sea –
Mistress, she yoked us like oxen to till her plot...
Her plot? Her *acre* – from morn till dark, and we
Thinking all done this-one-more appalling day,
Ready to sink and pant ourselves to sleep,
'How now?... My midnight whip! Bestir!' quoth she...
All morn, all afternoon t'was 'A-AA and ARRR-RE –'
How hard, how hard to the task – yet patient – she.
Damn! From her sea she took us, blew in our faces,
Now patted, now tanned our hides, and with her stick
Pointed at stones in the path, and counted the stones
And made her a pyramid, and we the while
Wretchedly, patiently went, constrained like a pair

Of oxen, *bueyes*, *boves*, fished from our zones
Of roach, dace, bream, skate, tench – does a minnow *spin*?
Must Ashanti's Cat-Fish *read*?
                              Nothing but computations!
Madame is in her smock like some grand *bouvier*
With a whip (how gladly... ha!... t'would encircle the nations:
'Come here, go there' could it but). And even the sun,
And even the spring of a 3-in-the-afternoon,
Banging all hammer-made to get into the room...
'No, no, *not now*...' You'd have thought she was stitching a doom:
'The plot must be *squared*, and *sown*, *and finished* quoth she.
With her wine she made us dizzy, yet worse with fatigue...
Our customary hither-and-yon? *Subjected to discipline*!
'Up from the Fen, ye sluggards' – thus quoth she,
'Get thee to school by an Emmet, Shakespeare said;
The tiny Ant, and the Warrior, and also the Bee,
The Wasp and the Hornet labour: *and so do we*;
On, little team, on, on!' At this we went
Pele mele in fury, fin over tip, half-drowned
Pashing through oozy clumps, traipsing that bloody plough;
Now pale, now puce were we, snuffling 'revenge',
Rambunctious and tougher than ever, puffing scorn
At one who sets a pen where tis not meant
To assay another's art – Tom's dagger on wood,
Bill's blade on marble – 'This *prose* must be exact!'
No no! Such yokes are jokes – we Fishes said.

'I shall do this again, however' – we heard –
'In the fullest plenitude of doubt, no doubt;
Agreed: tis not US, this acre, not for us three,
Yet on, on, on!'
                  At last she let us go;
We found the watery shadows on the wall
And flung ourselves therein on the scud of a curse.

Mistress, she took our work; with the point of a pin
She pricked some more, *alone*, and swilled her fill

Of those 'midnight oils' – pah! – slept. Then a whisper swam
Down the nervous current – ha! – of 'the vasty deep':
'To our dallying way again – arise and come
Back to our Cupe and Tongues – the acre is done!'

'Come, Liberating Wine!'

Come, liberating wine, up to the brim,
And ease the knots of time, that I may see
Something within the nod of destiny,
Dark, clear, or slow, or swift, or sharp or dim,
Looking not deep, not long, such may not be
With safety done, yet surely, rapidly.

Ay, he who talks too much may miss his road,
He who talks ill will surely lose his load,
And he who thinks and thinks and never speaks –
Poor carl – knows all too well now the heart breaks
Against the silent rocks, *tou-te la vie*.

Out of the wine what's possible may come true;
And that's not said alone for me and you,
For all tis said who drin the wine, pardie.

Oath – History Repeats

'By the black blood out of the mouth of God,
In time of waiting, man, do what you can!'
So run the words, and ay, for ever ran
Since half was lost and half put under sod.

From Prison

The doors will open and the gate swing wide,
With all God's music right by thy side,
And in the drapes of the evening breeze,
Wilt find thy love and gain thine ease,
              My honey-lamb, my darling.

You

To Steve

'I am that mystery that men call: the brain;
And I am tall and real, a heady truth;
My inspiration is nor age nor youth
But splicing of the hand and mind. Again,
I am the slant shaft angling for response,
The laugh in the honey seen against the sun;
Yet more, the full of shade when day is done –
Dawn am I not (love's enemy). And once
The tide of China shocked with Afric's blood
In me. I am the majesty of this,
The skull, the form, the all that holds the kiss
For you, against the time of fullest flood.
I am the rage, the temper of the hour,
The sapient waiting soil that is man's floor.'

Notes to the Poems

Outlaws

'If the End Be Now?...' first appeared in *The English Review*, September 1920, pp. 195–197. Nancy is credited as 'Nancy Fairbairn', her married name.

'Wheels' first appeared in *Wheels: An Anthology of Verse*, ed. Edith Sitwell (Oxford: Blackwell, 1916).

'Zeppelins' appears in *Wheels* as 'Destruction' with the following changes. Line 6 reads 'poorer, humbler, houses' and the final line reads 'To mock Death – laughing at their bitter pain.'

'Sonnet' first appeared in *Wheels* but with this final couplet: 'But Death has beaten him, and takes the pride / From the strong hands that held us till we died.'

'Promise' was published in *Wheels* as 'The Carnivals of Peace' and appears in *Outlaws* with a few minor changes. The most significant of these is the replacement of 'barren' with 'troubled' in the line 4.

'Mood' appears in *Wheels* as 'From the Train'. NC dates the poem 1915 in her manuscripts and states that it also appeared 'in one of the London reviews'.

'Prayer' first appeared in *The Eton College Chronicle* in 1915 and in *The New Age* (under her married name Nancy Fairbairn) November 1918, Volume 24, Issue 1.

'Answer to a Reproof' first appeared in *The English Review* as 'In Answer to a Reproof', October 1919, pp. 292–293.

Sublunary

NC's annotated manuscript of poems from *Sublunary* indicates places and dates of composition, as well as any previous publications. These are: **'In a Café'**: 'In a café at Pereigeux, or Limoges, Spring, 1921.' According to NC this poem and 'Eusebius Doubts' were published together in *The Observer*, London, 12 June 1921. **'Eusebius Doubts'**: 'In a café in Cahors, Spring 1921.' **'Iris of Memories'** refers to NC's

childhood friend, the poet, actress, playwright and artist's model Iris
Tree (1897–1968). Tree was the daughter of Sir Herbert Beerbohm,
actor and theatre manager. Cunard and Tree's friendship was signif-
icant during NC's youth and they lived together briefly in London
and travelled to Paris. Her poems appeared in *Poetry Review, The
New Age, The Athenaeum, Poetry* and several other publications during
the 1920s and 30s. Her collection *The Traveller and Other Poems*
appeared in 1927. For more on Tree's life see Daphne Fielding's *The
Rainbow Picnic: A Portrait of Iris Tree* (1974). '**Memory at the Fair**'
comp. 1920, pub. *The Observer*, 9 July 1922. '**Bottles, Mirrors and
Alchemy**': '1920 or later?'. '**Sonnet**' ('**Not till the fruit is gold upon
the tree**') comp. Provence, c. Autumn 1921, pub. *The Saturday Review*,
2 September 1922). '**At Les Baux**' comp. 1921, pub. *The Observer*, 11
December 1921. '**To Vaucluse Came Petrarch and Laura**' comp.
Provence, Autumn 1921, pub. *The Observer*, 7 December 7 1922.
'**Saintes Maries-De-La-Mer**' comp. 1921. '**The Night in Avignon**'
comp. 1921. '**Red Earth, Pale Olive, Fragmentary Vine**' and '**Pale
Moon, Slip of Malachite**' (comp. 1921) were condensed by NC into
one poem of two numbered parts entitled 'Mediterranean – From
the Var' in her Bodleian/Augustan Manuscript (1944). '**The Solitary**'
comp. c. 1921, pub. *The New Statesman*, 28 Oct 1922. '**Toulonnaise**' is
very likely a reference to NC's first governess who was from Toulon.
'**Allegory**' comp. Summer 1922 at The Mill House, Hungerford, pub.
The Saturday Review, 6 Jan 1923. NC notes that 'this number of the
Review was reproduced in miniature for the Queen's Doll's House
designed by Lutyens.' '**From Afar**' comp. c. 1919–1920. '**What If the
Bell Is Loud?**' comp. Winter 1921, Sanary, Var, pub. *The Saturday
Review*, 1 July 1922. '**You Have Lit the Only Candle**' comp. Autumn
1921, Sanary, Var, pub. *The Saturday Review*, 20 May 1921; 'come' is
corrected to 'comes' in line 10. '**I Think of You**' appears as 'In the Fields'
in one of NC's manuscripts; comp. Summer 1922 at The Mill House,
Hungerford, pub. *The Saturday Review*, 22 July 1922. '**At Fuenter-
rabia in Spain**' comp. September 1922, Hendaye, France, pub. *The
Saturday Review*, 28 October 1922. '**To the Eiffel Tower Restau-
rant**' comp. date unknown. In a letter dated 12 August 1957 from
NC to the American academic and biographer of Ronald Firbank,
Miriam Benkovitz, she writes: 'Alas the Eiffel Tower Restaurant, such
a venue from 1914 or so till... yes, till when? Till the mid-thirties...
should be "gone". I wish you could have had a glimpse of it, or indeed
that we could have dinner there, you and I, as it was then. The place

still exists geographically: 1 Percy street, facing the gloomy length of Charlotte Street which ends by becoming Fitzroy Street and runs into that square. Maybe you might care to see it. It is now called "The White Tower", Greek, and very expensive I think. I was taken there to dinner during the war by Cyril Connolly, who, in the Wyndham Lewis room upstairs, after having insisted on a regular "champagne dinner", confessed to me with gusto that he was a SNOB. He said he really, but really, did get more pleasure out of being with a duchess (any duchess) than with…Picasso. Quelle candeur. I have not been there since. The room downstairs was entirely changed and all those huge brass pots and palms, behind which one sometimes sheltered or had the illusion of so doing, had long gone. Surely this place was the only one in London that concentrated, somehow, the English and continental essence of "avant-garde", and art, and bohemianism. Stulik, the Austrian patron, made masses of money, but he lost yet more through being kind, and through being drunk, and through family upsets, permanently. What he would not have had to tell you about Ronald – and in such vivid ways and words…' (Yale University, Beinecke Rare Book and Manuscript Library, Nancy Cunard Collection GEN MSS 438 box 1, folder 2.) **'I Am Not One For Expression'** comp. Summer 1922 at The Mill House, Hungerford, pub. *The New Statesman*, 16 December 1922.

NC's manuscript also includes a typed page that quotes a letter from George Moore of 21 Jan 1922 regarding *Sublunary*: 'I am writing to you with delight, for I know that your Poems mean a great deal to you, and I don't mean to stint my praise of them; for there is conviction in my heart of improvement. [NC's hand, in pencil: *In Sublunary*] you have succeeded in conveying an atmosphere of midnight mystery and the awed desire of the disciples to obtain some knowledge of things occult from the wizard. This poem is, whether by design or accident, an endeavour to create something outside yourself. You know my beliefs – that art cannot be altogether subjective, that even the most subjective poems, the most personal to the poet, must be recreated to some extent, and the example I like to give of this necessary objectifi- cation is: Lines written in dejection near Naples, Shelley. I think you showed me the poem I admire at Martin-Eglise, but in a less perfect state than it is at present. To make the poem a striking success you should still go over it. I accept, and with delight, the deliberate obscu- rities of Morris, The Blue Closet, for example, but your obscurities are not deliberate – they rise from pale or weak thinking, uncertain vision

[…]' Moore continues by arguing that certain lines be 're-forged' or 're-cast', paraphrasing her poems and finding a new meaning for the rest of 'Horns in the Valley': 'It seems to me, Nancy, that we have now had enough of the Opera, and that the next verses should tell your belief that the evocative horns are not real horns inasmuch as the love-adventure of Tristan and Isolda is not in a single brief moment in time, but an immortal moment carried on through eternity which in certain moods is audible to us.' (Nancy Cunard Papers, Harry Ransom Center, box 2, folder 9.)

Parallax

NC's archived manuscript carries the original title of 'The Sempiternal Fool'. NC also indicates that the poem was at least partly written in Italy in 1923, most likely the two sections she chose to reprint in the Bodleian / Augustan Manuscript of 1944, which is reproduced in *The Poems of Nancy Cunard: From the Bodleian Library*, Trent Editions, 2005 ('Dry moss […] no epitaph.' and 'Then I was in a train […] I had you to myself then.'). One typescript of the entire poem gives the address of her apartment at 2 Rue le Regrattier, Paris, so it seems likely that NC completed the poem in Paris and changed the title retrospectively.

Poems Two 1925

'In Provins' according to NC's notes was published in *The New Coterie*, London, no. 2, Spring 1926. 'Simultaneous' was written in Wans-ford-in-England, Autumn 1924 and first published in *The Outlook*, London, 13 Aug 1927 and in *The New Coterie*, No 6, London, Summer and Autumn number, 1927.

Relève into Maquis

Composed in London, February 1944 and published by Grasshopper Press, Derby, June 1944. Later, in the 1944 Bodleian / Augustan Manuscript, NC retitled the poem 'The Relève and the Maquis', and there are certain significant variants from stanza 2 onwards:

> And a mean wind blew doubt: 'Some of it's true?
> No, it is blackmail, lies.' And the months crept.
> '…Or perhaps one may claim a prisoner? Then if so

Three of us go, if Jean…?' But no. Meanwhile
One million and a quarter prisoners stay in the Reich;
In France comes hunger to sit between nerve and flesh,
Press-gangs for labour, food-cards taken away,
Reprisals on a wife, eight guillotines
Travel the land (till then there had been one),
Shootings and hitting back – But it's always: NO.

In July of '42 the first train comes,
La Relève out of Germany! Blazed in the traitor press,
Staged at Compiegne where Hitler signed and stamped
With fist and foot his Armistice sham as Fascism.
How many men in that train? Three hundred, packed
like a load of curses, sick, and half un-limbed.

He sat in a fireless kitchen head in hands
'From under our feet the ground… and France is done…
Is done? Is *down*. But I live. I'll fight against that.'
Just before dawn he unearthed the rabbit gun
And his old revolver blessed by Spain, and went –
To the high lands by the goat track, a wind of decision
Blowing dawn into day. 'Wife and life now these two…'
Gun and pistol under knee he sat after the four-hour trek
Till a boy surged calling 'Password?'
So the new rhythm began – 'We're not a hundred miles from Vichy'
'Nor a hundred months from freedom.' Thus into concourse
Of camp – some sixty, some of sixteen, but mainly those of the
                                                    young twenties:

Ceux du Maquis, francs-tireurs, partisans, guerillas,
'Refractories to law and order' Vichy calls them;
Into the Secret Army the months have made them.

Man Ship Tank Gun Plane

Dedicated to NC's friend the poet and editor of Ernest Benn's
Augustan poetry imprint, Edward John Thompson. Comp. March
1944 in East Chaldon, Dorchester, pub. by NC in Yeovil, Somerset,
22 April 1944 in an edition of 400. Variants of the title exist among
NC's manuscripts, including instances in which the letterspaces in
the title are replaced by '='s or '–'s. The notes to the Trent edition,

written by John Lucas, state that Alun Lewis and Nordahl Grieg were both poets who died whilst on active service in the 1940s.

From the Bodleian Manuscript

In a letter to Thomas Moult on 2 Dec 194[?], NC writes: 'I never met Katherine Mansfield, though I admired her writings very much indeed. Since all that time I have met Gurdjiev, in Paris; on another tack he was rather, and I did not like him at all. As to my own poems – there seems to be a good chance now of some of them being published, but I have not yet heard quite definitely. It would be a selection; only two or three of the older ones, and the rest poems since 1936, and some recent ones; some of them have appeared in the Statesman and other reviews here and abroad, some, never. Besides this I am getting them into final form, for a volume called "The Lands That Were Today". I think about 40, and very different indeed to the earlier days. Everything I have is in France, and probably gone for ever, as my house is in Normandy, and was looted. So everything being also out of print it seems a perfect caesura.' The manuscript in question is likely to be the one now held in the Edward Thompson papers at the Bodleian Library. The manuscript was meant for Thompson's *Augustan* modern poetry editions, but it never saw publication.

'Love's Alba against Time, Time's against Love': Comp. 1929. Lines 13–14 ('And as Aragon has it / Aima, ai-ma') are a quotation from Louis Aragon's 'Poem a crier dans les ruins' (1929), published around the time that Aragon's and Cunard's love affair ended.

'Love, Death, Time, Weather': Comp. 1929.

'Between Time and Etc': 'Dowson' refers to the poet Ernest Dowson (1867–1900).

'Tell It, Glen': Comp. May 1934 at Réanville. The Trent edition note suggests that this poem was written on the occasion of the fifth National Hunger March (Glasgow to London, January 1934).

'And Also Faustus': Comp. June 1935 at Réanville. NC's dedication and note: 'To Tristan Tzara, after his great speech on "The Meaning of the Poem in Life", at the 1st Writers Congress in Defence of Culture, June 24, 1935, in Paris.'

'Yes, It Is Spain': Comp. August 1937 at Réanville, pub. *Life and Letters Today*, October 1938. Translated into Spanish, pub. *Aurora de*

Chile, Santiago, Chile, summer 1940.

'To Eat Today': NC notes on the manuscript: 'Written during the air-raid of 13 Sept 1938, in the Hotel Majestic, Barcelona at lunch.' Pub. *The New Statesman*, 1 Oct 1938.

'Pamiatnik – Memorial of the Bittersweet': Comp. 1937, Réanville. In pencil NC has written at the bottom of the typescript: 'My house my house… Where are you now my house? June 1940.' Versions in Cunard's archive replace 'zone' with 'seam' in line 13.

'EOS': Comp. Paris 1938 and London 1943. Eos is the Greek goddess of dawn.

'Sequences from a Long Epic on Spain': Comp. 1937–39, according to NC's typescript table of contents. In one manuscript version, 'November Something' reads 'November '36' in 'December 1936, Madrid'. Curiously, the Trent edition does not include the section about the Republican aviator, in spite of its presence in the Bodleian manuscript. Perhaps the editors were concerned by the gruesome nature of the facts.

'The Lands That Were Today': Comp. September 1939 at Réanville. Kay Boyle (1902–1992) was an American poet, novelist, journalist, and political activist. Boyle and NC were close friends from 1923 onwards. For more on Boyle's life and work, see Thomas Austenfeld's *Kay Boyle for the Twenty-First Century: New Essays* (Trier: Wissenschaftlicher Verlag Trier, 2008) and Sandra Spanier's *Kay Boyle: Artist and Activist* (Carbondale: Southern Illinois University Press, 1986).

'Journey to the New World': NC's archived typescript bears the heading 'A later sequence in the Poem on Spain' and a possible composition date in NC's hand pencilled in the margin, 'July 1936'.

'The Chilean Sonnets': Comp. 1940. NC travelled to Chile in 1940 and it seems likely that these sonnets were written during or just after her visit. NC's note: 'In January 1939 a cataclysmic earthquake wrecked the town of Chillán, eight hours to the south of Santiago. When I was there a year and a half later, people still stood (in the rain) thinking: "how to rebuild?" Nothing can be more tragic than these ruins. Nothing? That very week the Germans were surging over France, laying new ruins on a gigantic scale. Of these things one would talk with the people of Chillán, and with the warm-hearted *rotos* of Chile.

The *roto* is the name given to the poor man of Chile, the descendant of the Indians and the Conquistadores; literally "the broken one". The poet is Arturo Gardoqui, one of Chile's most lyrical poets. I have seen the ruins of the house in which he was buried alive, seen them with him. But soon we were forgetting all this for the anguish of France; it was in June, 1940. (June 6, 1940. Concón, Pacific. Chile.) "Amaranth of Sunset": (1940) (*Mijito*: my very dear, a Chillenism)'.

'Psalm for Trinidad': included in NC's book *Psalm of the Palms*. NC's notes indicate that the poem was composed in 'Maraval, Trinidad, Feb. La Havana, Cuba, July 1941. This and the following three sonnets were privately published in an edition of 50 in La Habana, Cuba, in July 1941.'

'"How Long?" Is Not "For Ever"': Comp. according to NC's notes in 'Barbados, March 1941. Published in a West Indian paper at the time.'

'Less Than the Slave': NC's note indicates the poem was written at 'Wilhelmstad, Curacoa, May, 1941. Remembering Lily in the cocoa-woods in Trinidad.'

'To Alfred Cruickshank': Comp. Maraval, Trinidad, January 1941. NC notes: 'Published in *The People*, Trinidad, and a Teacher's Journal, at the time.)' Alfred Cruickshank (1880–1940) was a Trinidadian poet.

'14 Juillet 1941': NC notes on her manuscript that '(Victor Hugo is loved in Cuba by the people, for he protested against the continuation of slavery there in many of his writings. There is a bust of him, with some words of his in one of the little squares in El Vedado, Habana. Here, this 14ᵗʰ of July 1941, after an immense demonstration in the streets in honour of France, they brought flowers, mainly red flowers, to Victor Hugo.)'

'Fragment in the Old World': Comp. December 1941 in London. An earlier typescript is titled 'Walking in Craven St, Strand': '(A short series called "Nights". For Morris Gilbert, "Whiles absence".' This is most likely the American journalist, Morris Gilbert, with whom Cunard was in a relationship in the 1940s.

'Incarnations': Comp. February–November 1942 in London. In a letter to Miriam Benkovitz, NC remarks that the poem was 'written to, and of, such a dear, beloved man, American, whom I knew then well.' A typescript of the poem reads 'Love Poem' and then in NC's hand: 'For and to Morris'.

'Whose Desert?': Comp. November 1942 in London. NC notes: 'The Moors of Spanish Morocco have twice been involved in wars since the beginning of this century against Spain. The war of the Riff which lasted over 20 years and could only be won by Spain due to French aid, waged by the Spanish Monarchist regime against the Arabs, and detested by the soldiers and masses of the Spanish people. Then the war of Fascist Intervention, led by Franco and other rebel generals, which bled Spanish Morocco dry of men and sent scores of thousands of them to their death against the Spanish Republicans in a war execrated by them. The roumis are the "foreigners". Hussein is in the fighting against the Germans in Tunisia. Accidiae are certain evil spirits in Arab lore. The Shott Jerid is a huge, impressive, now-dry, now-watery salt-marsh. (I have been in it with Norman Douglas.) Maitre Tahar is a Tunisian Arab lawyer musing on Darlan and Allied policy and on the future of his country, a protectorate (in rags) of France.'

'Dordogne': NC's note reads: '(1930, 1943) *Maquisards*: Those who have taken to the *maquis*, the wilds; in this case the *cause* – to defy the Nazis' and Vichy's order to go to forced labour in Germany. Today thousands are in the *maquis* in various parts of France, many of them in the Limousin, the region around much of the Dordogne river. Often they have defeated the armed guards, German and Vichy, sent to bring them in by force. They are organised, helped by the population of whatever region they are in.'

Previously Unpublished or Uncollected Poems

'Soldiers Fallen in Battle': NC's first published poem. *The Eton College Chronicle*, June 1916. Comp. 1915 and published alongside 'Sonnet' ('This is no time for prayer or words or song…').

'Remorse' and 'Uneasiness': Comp. 1915–1916. Originally published in *Wheels* (Oxford: Blackwell Books, 1916), ed. Edith Sitwell.

'Brigit': On a typed copy of the poem NC has written: 'Sent Derek and Brigit Feb 22, 1965'. Possibly this poem is for Brigit Patmore, the poet Richard Aldington's one-time companion.

'Victor and Nancy at Pertenhall': NC notes that this is 'A sort of letter – though to whom? 7 days later I knew, for you were here, Rosemary,

how unexpectedly!' Comp. at Villa Pomone in Saint-Jean-Cap-
Ferrat, 'with music playing, night, Dec 21, 1963, at one go'.

'Pain Sonnets': These are likely comp. 1964, whilst NC was conva-
lescing after a fall and leg surgery. Around this time, in January
1964, NC began her proposed long poem 'The Visions' (or 'Cosmo's
Dream'). In her manuscripts she writes about what might be these
pain sonnets, intended at one time to be part of 'The Visions': 'And
not here, but typed already, half of the pages in pre-final order, are the
very many sequences of the long poem "The Visions", which began
to be written immediately after leg accident – including the sonnet
on Pain and the two others on pain. David Garnett had been, from
distant parts of Spain, to visit Clive Bell in Mentone and came to see
me at Pomone. We talked about poetry and about what I was writing
then. Reflectively he said "not many poets have written about pain".'

'To Professor Bernelot Moens': Comp. 7 July 1934 at Réanville.

'To Douglas Cooper from Nancy Cunard': Comp. 3 Jan 1964 at Villa
Pomone. Douglas Cooper (1911–1984) was a British art critic and
friend of NC's.

'For Douglas Cooper': Comp. early December 1963 at Villa Pomone.
Sent to Cooper, with a note, 8 Dec 1963.

'Passport to Freedom': NC's note on the typescript: 'In "Passport to
Freedom" (temporary title of unfinished book of poems to 6 countries).
Lindsay Drummond said he would publish it, I F enough subscriptions
were to come in. I wanted the photo-montages of the superb German
Hertzfield (John Heartfield) one to each poem. (Nov 16.) "France"
was published in *The New Statesmen*, Jan 17, 1942. "Italy" (the 2 first
sonnets only in *The New Statesman*" (see date elsewhere). "Russia" was
published in a special folder made by John St John Woods, for sale for
aid to Russia (Mrs Churchill's), early in 1942 (?). "Spain" likewise. There
would not have been much more to it than what stands here: "Soldier,
poor soldier" sequence. As for the poem to the USA, I got no further
than the beautiful, classical known line of "Up from the grassy roots".'
The typescript table of contents of *Passport to Freedom* '1941–42–43
London' lists them in order: 'France Qui dit Haine di Resistance' then
U.S.S.R, then Italy, then Spain, Germany, England, U.S.A.'

'France': Comp. 16 November 1941 in London. Dedicated to

Louis Aragon. Published in translation in *Poemes a la France*, Seghers, Paris, 1947.

'Italy' 1: Comp. London, 28 November–30 December 1941. NC notes this was published in *The New Statesman*, May 1942.

'Italy' 2: Comp. 30 December 1941–22 February 1942 in London.

'Italy' 3: NC notes this was published in *New Times*, May 1942.

'Russia – The U.S.S.R.': Comp. 19 January 1942 in London.

'Spain': NC's typescript notes: 'dedicated to Spain and to Sam Wild'.

'Germany': NC notes that this was published in *Life and Letters Today*, London, Summer 1943.

'England': NC notes that this poem is written 'In the dialect, more or less, or rather, in the accent of the Leicestershire Midlands. 21–22 March, Wansford. 1942.' She adds the performance note: 'The "Soldier, poor soldier", between each line should be done in drum-taps. Till the last one ends on a different note of the drum.'

'The Poet to His Wars': Comp. April 1962 in Toulouse. John Gawsworth (1912–1970) was a British poet and anthologist who served in the Royal Air Force during World War II.

'Three Prison Sonnets': Comp. 21 February–2 March in Palma, Mallorca. Solita Solano (1888–1975) was a poet and journalist and good friend of NC. NC was in Palma at various times between 1957 and 1960.

'By Their Faces Shall Ye Know Them': typescript dated 26 February, Palma.

'In the Watches of the Night': Comp. Spring 1960 in England.

'Order': Comp. 26 April 1960, Café Royal in London.

'To Whom?': Comp. 9 May 1960 in London.

'Portrait-Sonnet': Comp. 9 May 1960 in London.

'8 AM Sonnet': Comp. 16 June 1960 at Holloway Sanatorium, Virginia Water.

'From Afar': Comp. 1919–1920. NC notes that this poem was published in an English or American Review but does not give the title.

'Of Liberty': Comp. 1920 or 1921, pub. *The Saturday Review*, 18 August 1923.

'Saintes De La Mer': Possible comp. date pencilled in NC's hand is 1921.

'Aigues Mortes': Pub. *The Nation and Athenaeum*, London, 14 May 1921.

'Transimene': Comp. March 1923 in Cortona, pub. *The Saturday Review*, 2 June 1923.

'When We Must Go Our Ways': Possible comp. date given as 1921, pub. *The Saturday Review*, 28 Oct 1922.

'The Solitary': Possible comp. date given as 1921, pub. *The New Statesman*, 28 Oct 1922.

'The White Cat': Comp. Summer 1923 at Varengeville, Normandy, pub. *The Best Poems of 1924*, ed. L. A. G. Strong, Boston, USA.

'Wansford Bridge Spring': Comp. March 1923, Wansford, England.

'Looking at a Photograph in the Same Dress 1928–1926': Comp. Christmas 1928 in Paris. NC notes that this poem is 'for Henry', most likely the jazz musician Henry Crowder.

'For December': Comp. December 1928 at Réanville. The poem is an acrostic of 'HENRY'.

'1929's Spring Poem': Comp. March 1929 at Réanville.

'The Boeuf Blues': Comp. in Paris 1929 or 1930, dedicated in NC's notes to Henry [Crowder]. This poem also appeared in *Henry-Music* as 'Memory Blues' (Réanville: The Hours Press, 1930).

'The Chilean Sonnets': Comp. 9 June 1940 in Concón, Pacifico, Chile. NC also notes that *Mijito* is 'A Chileanism: My dear'.

'Equatorial Way': Comp. 1930 at Réanville, pub. *Henry-Music* (The Hours Press, December 1930) and *The Crisis* (New York, February 1931).

'Southern Sheriff': This poem first appeared in the *Negro Anthology*, ed. Nancy Cunard (1934), in the Poetry section subtitled 'by White Poets' which included poems by Alfred Kreymborg, Louis Zukofsky, and William Plomer, among others.

'Rape': NC's papers include the following note. 'London, June 1933, Published in one of my leaflets for Scottsboro Defense that summer. And in "The Afro-American", October 7, 1933.' 'To Haywood Patterson in jail, framed up on the vicious "rape" lie, twice condemned to death, despite conclusive and maximum proof of his innocence – and to the eight other Scottsboro boys. June, 1933 (In the American Southern States, after Emancipation changed the Negro's status from that of a white master's valuable property to one of uttermost economic and social serfdom, the favourite charge brought against him is the lie of "raping white women". It operates somewhat in the way I have written it here, which leads to an actual or a "legal" lynching.)'

'At Dawn': Comp. 9 June, 1940 at Concón, Pacifico, Chile.

'June for Freedom – June for Italy': Comp. June 11, 1944.

'Réanville': NC explains the origin of the poem: 'Just returned to Paris, Hadley Mowrer (first wife of Ernest Hemingway and wife now of Paul Scott Mowrer, brother of Edgar Ansell Mowrer, specialist on Germany) says she is spending her days shaking out the curtains of the E. A. Mowrer flat in the Rue de l'Universite, uninhabited since the war began. She says it all smells of cheese. And I am in Normandy, in my once house. July 15, 1945.' 'Rue Jadin, Night, July 15, 1945, Paris'.

'In the Studio': Comp. 1923 in Eugene McCown's Paris studio on the Rue Campagne Première, while he was painting her portrait.

'In San Gimignano': NC's typescript of the poem notes that it was composed in the Hotel Flora, Frascati on the night of 31 January. She adds that she's 'remembering the day in San Gimignano at the beginning of December 1952', giving the poem a probable composition date.

'June for Italy – June For Freedom': Comp. 11 June 1944. On NC's typescript there is also a small map of southern Italy indicating the movement of an expanding military offensive. For Gawsworth see note to 'The Poet to His Wars', above.

'Kikuyu': Comp. November 1952 at Bordighera.

'Jaime': Comp. dawn, 3 February 1960 at Hotel Inglés, Valencia.

'Late-Night Sonnet': Comp. in bed on 5 November 1962 at Hotel Divan, Gourdon, Lot, France. According to NC 'Mart' is a reference to Chaucer's name for war.

'Letter': Comp. 7 January 1965 (additional typescript is dated 9 January 1965). Cunard's biographer, Lois Gordon, incorrectly refers to this as a 'prose poem'. For a discussion of the poem and its dedicatee, refer to the Introduction.

'Lincoln': Comp. 'in the United States, Summer 1932', pub. *The Daily Gleaner*, Jamaica, 21 July 1932.

'The Love Story': Comp. date on typescript is given as 1919.

'¿Me Oyes, Mijito?': Comp. April 1940, Santiago, Chile.

'Mosley 1943': Comp. 25 November 1943, Half-Moon Street, London.

'Myself': Comp. August 1919, Turks Croft, Sussex.

'And an Afternoon': Comp. according to NC's notes 'In a Lyons near the Strand, London, 5 March 1942.'

'April, 1942': Comp. April 1942, Queen Street, London.

'Saturday Night in "The Golden Lion"': Comp. October 1942, London. Nina Hamnett (1890–1956) was a Welsh artist and writer. his poem appears to be part of the sequence 'Nights'.

'October–November Night in "The Coach & Horses"': Comp. London 1942. This poem also appears to be part of the sequence 'Nights'.

'Of a Glass Stopper Found in the Sea at Collioure s. w. France, in 1951': Comp. end of July 1961, Lamothe, France. Valentine Ackland (1906–1969) was an English poet and the partner of Sylvia Townsend-Warner.

'Pisces Pulled Plough': Comp. 26–28 February 1953 in Frascati, Italy.

'"Come, Liberating Wine!"': Comp. 4 January at Café Bellver, Hotel Cannes, and 5 Jan 1960 in Palma, Spain.

'Oath – History Repeats': Comp. 3 February 1960 in Valencia, Spain.

'By Their Faces Shall Ye Known Them': Comp. 26 February in Palma, Spain.

'From Prison': Comp. 14 March 1960 in Valencia, Spain.

'You': Comp. January 1941, Maraval, Trinidad.

Further Reading

Works by Nancy Cunard

Outlaws (London: Elkin Matthews, 1921)

Sublunary (London: Hodder and Stoughton, 1923)

Parallax (London: Hogarth Press, 1925)

Poems Two 1925 (London: Aquila Press, 1930)

Relève into Maquis (Derby: Grasshopper Press, 1944)

Man–Ship–Tank–Gun–Plane. A Poem (London, n.p., 1944)

Poems of Nancy Cunard: From the Bodleian Library, ed. John Lucas (Nottingham: Trent Editions, 2005)

Henry-Music, ed. Nancy Cunard (Paris: The Hours Press, 1930)

Black Man and White Ladyship, An Anniversary (London: The Utopia Press, 1931)

Negro: An Anthology, ed. Nancy Cunard (London: Wishart & Co., 1934)

Authors Take Sides on the Spanish Civil War, ed. Nancy Cunard (London: Left Review, 1937)

The White Man's Duty: An Analysis of the Colonial Question, with George Padmore (London: W. H. Allen, 1942)

Poems for France: Written by British Poets on France Since the War (London: La France Libre, 1944), published in French as *Poèmes à la France* (Paris: Pierre Seghers, 1944)

Nous Gens D'Espagne (Perpignan: Imprimerie Labau, 1949)

Grand Man: Memories of Norman Douglas (London: Secker and Warburg, 1954)

G.M.: Memories of George Moore (London: Rupert Hart-Davis, 1956)

These Were the Hours: Memories of My Hours Press, 1928–1931, ed. Hugh Ford (Carbondale: Southern Illinois University Press, 1969)

Thoughts About Ronald Firbank, foreword by Miriam J. Benkovitz (New York: Albondocani Press, 1971)

Essays on Race and Empire, ed. Maureen Moynagh (Ormskirk: Broadview, 2002)

Les poètes du monde défendent le peuple espagnol, ed. Pablo Neruda and Nancy Cunard (Réanville: The Hours Press, 1937), republished in Spanish as *Los poetas del mundo defienden al pueblo español* (Seville: Renacimiento, 2002/2010)

Selected Works about Nancy Cunard

Mulk Raj Anand, *Conversations in Bloomsbury* (London: Wildwood House, 1981)

David Ayers, 'The Waste Land, Nancy Cunard and Mina Loy', in *Modernism: A Short Introduction* (Oxford: Blackwell, 2004)

Anthony Barnett, *Listening for Henry Crowder: A Monograph on His Almost Lost Music* (Lewes: Allardyce & Barnett, 2007)

Shari Benstock, *Women of the Left Bank* (Austin: University of Texas Press, 1986)

Anne Chisholm, *Nancy Cunard: A Biography* (London: Sidgwick & Jackson, 1979)

Henry Crowder, *As Wonderful as All That?: Henry Crowder's Memoir of His Affair with Nancy Cunard 1928–1935* (Navarro, California: Wild Trees Press, 1987)

James Donald, *Some of These Days: Black Stars, Jazz Aesthetics, and Modernist Culture* (Oxford: Oxford University Press, 2015)

Jane Dowson, *Women, Modernism and British Poetry, 1910–1939: Resisting Femininity* (Aldershot: Ashgate, 2002)

Daphne Winifred Fielding, *Emerald and Nancy: Lady Cunard and her Daughter* (London: Eyre & Spottiswoode, 1968)

Susan Stanford Friedman, 'Nancy Cunard', in Bonnie Kime-Scott, ed., *The Gender of Modernism* (Bloomington: Indiana University Press, 1990)

Hugh Ford, ed., *Nancy Cunard: Brave Poet, Indomitable Rebel, 1896–1965.* (Philadelphia: Chilton Book Co., 1968)

Lois Gordon, *Nancy Cunard: Heiress, Muse, Political Idealist* (New York: Columbia University Press, 2007)

Maroula Joannou, 'Nancy Cunard's English Journey', in *Feminist Review*, 78, 2004

Jane Marcus, *Hearts of Darkness: White Women Write Race* (New Brunswick, NJ: Rutgers University Press, 2003)

Maureen Moynagh, 'Cunard Lines: Political Tourism and its Texts', *New Formations* 34 (Summer, 1998), pp. 70–90

Michael North, *The Dialect of Modernism: Race, Language & Twentieth-Century Literature* (Oxford: Oxford University Press, 1994)

Laura Winkiel, *Modernism, Race and Manifestos* (Cambridge: Cambridge University Press, 2008)

Laura Winkiel, 'Nancy Cunard's *Negro* and the Transnational Politics of Race', *Modernism/Modernity*, vol. 13.3, 2006

Acknowledgements

I am grateful for the assistance and support staff at the Harry Ransom Center, University of Texas, Austin Libraries. In particular, I am indebted to the wisdom, guidance, and patience of Richard Watson and his team. Additional research libraries (and their excellent staff) that accommodated my visits and requests include Oxford's Bodleian Library, Yale University's Beinecke Rare Book Room, and King's College (Cambridge).

Without the enthusiastic support of Michael Schmidt at Carcanet this book – and the reprinted works of other important modernists – would not have been possible. I am fortunate to have been awarded an AHRC/BBC Radio 3 New Generation Thinker award, which has provided a platform for sharing Nancy Cunard's work and incredible life with a wider audience. I am also indebted to the University of Liverpool for providing me with the time to complete this volume.

One of the great joys of this project has been meeting those with passionate knowledge of either Cunard or her many contexts. My thanks to Maroula Joannou, Jane Dowson, Kathy Mezei, Tory Young, the late Jane Marcus and, not least, Anthony Barnett, whose encyclopedic work on Henry Crowder deserves the highest praise. A dedicated group of Cunardians became known to me as I was working on this edition. I have benefited from being in touch with Adam Ghanii, Rachel Farebrother, and Jenny Greenshields, and I hope to carry on those conversations about their own remarkable research.

My thanks to Stuart Rawlinson for his invaluable assistance in transcribing these poems from various sources and for his sharp, academic eye. And to James Byrne, as always, for his invaluable advice and support.